"People don't take trips—
trips take people."

John Steinbeck, the writer who first inspired
WILDSAM, wrote those words in his American
epic *Travels with Charley*. They capture the core
belief of the book you now hold in your hands:
That unforgettable experiences are born from the
unexpected. And road trips, most especially, beg the
traveler to write plans in pencil and trace routes
on the fly. May the stories in these pages stoke
this kind of adventure.

WILDSAM
FIELD GUIDES

WILDSAM FIELD GUIDES™

Copyright © 2020

All rights reserved. No portion of this
book may be reproduced in any form without
permission from the publisher.

Published in the United States
by Wildsam Field Guides, Austin, Texas.

ISBN 978-1-4671-9901-8

Illustrations by Bijou Karman

To find more field guides, please visit
www.wildsam.com

CONTENTS

Discover the people and places that tell the story of California

WELCOME

_____

ON OUR LAST TRIP to Big Sur, when we parked at the Ernst Ewoldsen Nature Center, the feeling in the air was peculiar. The river burbled nearby, summer birds talked in the trees, the thick sagey dampness cooled us as we funneled toward the trailhead. All that was pretty normal. Big Sur has a way of being casual in its glory. No, this was an uneasy serenity, equal doses of giddiness and dislocation as we switchbacked through the redwoods.

We were walking [the only way in] to a different Big Sur: "the Island," as residents called it. It was August 2017, after two monstrous landslides along Highway 1. The first took out Pfeiffer Canyon Bridge, half a mile down from where we stood. The second big slide was at Mud Creek, about 35 miles south. Other than a few construction trucks and the occasional helicopter drop at Post Ranch Inn, the place felt deserted, the infamous car traffic gone.

Hundreds of years ago, explorers on ships from Spain and other places actually thought all of California was an island. Maps from the 1500s show it either set apart, floating out in the Pacific, or sometimes half-drawn, a mysterious phantom of a place. Rebecca Solnit, in her book _A Field Guide to Getting Lost_, describes one such map, where "the west coast begins to dissolve where California starts ... as though the world there was not yet made."

Fantasy has defined California's essence ever since. Even when the first grizzled settlers found no riches in them hills, the first ingénue failed to grace the silver screen or the first coders left Menlo Park without owning a single foosball table. Even in disappointment, California offers itself as an archipelago. Yosemite for Muir. City Lights Books for so many. Laurel Canyon. Salvation Mountain. Even Disneyland, an island of childhood.

Henry Miller lived in Big Sur for almost 20 years. He called it the place that taught him to say amen. That summer day in 2017, as we hiked up to empty Highway 1, found our way to Nepenthe and settled onto the sundeck for Ambrosia burgers, we felt the same. Alone, alive, lost and found. —The Editors

ESSENTIALS

Trusted intel and
traveler info about iconic
statewide culture and practices

PLANNING

CAMPER
Texino
Los Angeles
texino.com

. . . .

CANOE
Burke's Canoe Trips
Forestville
burkescanoetrips.com

. . . .

HOUSEBOAT
Lake Shasta
houseboats.com

. . . .

ELECTRIC BIKE
Adventures in Cycling
Sonoma and Napa
winecountrycyclingtours.com

. . . .

AIRSTREAM
Roam & Board
Throughout SoCal
roamandboard.us

. . . .

RAFT
Raft California
American, Yuba, Truckee
and other rivers
raftcalifornia.com

. . . .

SKATEBOARD
Jay's Rentals Venice Beach
Venice
jaysrentalsvb.com

CLIMATE

California is hot and dry, also foggy and wet, also buried in snow, also blasted by warm Santa Ana winds, also on fire, at least sometimes. Which of those you get depends on whether you're in the Mediterranean climate of the coastal and southern parts, or the parched hills inland, or the misty forests up north. Wherever you are, true summer doesn't start till fall.

CALENDAR

JAN	Tết Festival, *Los Angeles*
	Rose Parade, *Pasadena*
FEB	Firefall, *Yosemite*
MAR	Film Noir Festival, *Los Angeles*
APR	Coachella, *Indio*
MAY	Calaveras County Fair & Jumping Frog Jubilee, *Angels Camp*
JUN	Pride Parade, *San Francisco*
JUL	California Rodeo, *Salinas*
AUG	Accordion Festival, *Cotati*
	US Open of Surfing, *Huntington Beach*
SEP	Wasteland Weekend, *Edwards*
OCT	Hardly Strictly Bluegrass, *San Francisco*
NOV	Sandhill Crane Festival, *Lodi*
DEC	Christmas Boat Parade, *Newport Beach*

GEOGRAPHY

Notable terrain formations and where to find them.

KELP FOREST
Dense seaweed clusters shelter more than 1,000 marine species on rocky reefs. *Channel Islands National Park*

....

SALT FLAT
Dried sodium crystals blanket an arid basin, 282 feet below sea level. *Badwater Basin, Death Valley National Park*

FAULT LINES
More than 500 active faults criss-cross the state, yielding quakes every three minutes *San Andreas, Carrizo Plain*

....

CHAPARRAL HILLS
Brush and scrub dominate Southern California's foothills and mountain slopes. *Crestridge Ecological Reserve, El Cajon*

REDWOOD FORESTS
The tallest living things on Earth, some coast red-woods date to the Roman Empire. *Redwood National Park, Orick*

....

TIDE POOLS
Sea stars, goose-neck barnacles, periwinkle snails and more dot the rocky coastline. *Fitzgerald Marine Reserve, Moss Beach*

FOODWAYS

History, culture and tradition in a dish.

Burrito — Stuffed with fries, supersized or doused with salsa, "little donkeys" first appeared in the 1930s. *Nico's Mexican Food, San Diego*

Fig — Plump, sweet, inward-blooming florets, figs grow in eight varieties in fertile San Joaquin Valley and are fresh from June to November. *Trelio, Clovis*

Cioppino — Gold Rush-era stew made with Dungeness crab, clams, mussels, squid in tomato-based broth. Crusty sourdough on the side. *Duarte's Tavern, Pescadero*

Martini — Cocktail historians trace the gin- and vermouth-based "elixir of quietude" to Northern California, circa 1860. *Aub Zam Zam, San Francisco*

HISTORY

1400s... Diverse native tribes flourish

1542 ..... First Spanish tall ships anchor in San Diego Bay

1804...... Spain governs Alta California province, followed by Mexico

1823...... In Sonoma, final of 21 Franciscan missions built

1881 ..... Prospectors find silver in Calico, start 15-year boom

1892 ..... First meeting of Sierra Club alpinists, Muir presides

1907 ..... Santa Cruz boardwalk and park opens

1924...... Last sighting of a California grizzly bear, in Sequoia NP

1932...... Pilot spots giant, mysterious geoglyph figures near Blythe

1937...... Big Sur stretch of U.S. 1 completed by San Quentin prisoners

1940..... Steinbeck's *The Grapes of Wrath* wins Pulitzer Prize

1946..... *The Hollywood Reporter* column starts blacklisting movement

1947 ..... Chuck Yeager breaks sound barrier over Mojave

1948..... In-N-Out Burger opens in Baldwin Park

1949..... Hollywood coffee shop [Googies] inspires futuristic trends

1955...... Disneyland opens in Anaheim

1956 ..... Eames' lounge chair and ottoman created in Venice Beach

1958 ..... Wham-O sells 25 million Hula-Hoops in four months

1965 ..... Psychedelic quintet plays as Grateful Dead at Ken Kesey home

..... Riots erupt in Watts neighborhood in Los Angeles

1968..... Robert Kennedy shot, killed at LA's Ambassador Hotel

1969..... 100,000 barrels of oil spill into Santa Barbara Channel

1978..... Harvey Milk, first openly gay elected official, assassinated

1982 ..... *E.T.* becomes top-grossing film of all time [till '93 *Jurassic Park*]

1984...... Carl Lewis wins four gold medals in Summer Olympics

1989 ..... Earthquake delays World Series game in Bay Area

1992 .... Johnny Carson's 4,531st and final *Tonight Show* episode

1997 ..... Steve Jobs returns [after being fired in 1985] to Apple

2000 .... Screaming Eagle's '92 Cab Sauv sells at charity auction for $500,000

.... Dot-com bubble bursts

2007..... Thomas Keller's The French Laundry given three Michelin stars

2014...... World's largest solar power station opens in Mojave Desert

2018 ..... Ranch Fire, near Ukiah, is largest in state's history

MEDIA

BOOKS

☞ *There There* by Tommy Orange: Gertrude Stein's oft-repeated words about Oakland inspired the title of this debut novel, in which 12 Native Americans grapple with identity, dispossession and tradition in present-day East Bay.

....

☞ *Parable of the Sower* by Octavia E. Butler: The first in the "Earthseed" series opens in a dystopian Los Angeles ravaged by climate change and inequality, from which a hyper-empathetic heroine ventures north to establish a new way of life.

....

☞ *California: A History* by Kevin Starr: The late historian explains how California became the world's fifth-largest economy and a prime cultural exporter, examining its dark failures as closely as its bright achievements.

....

☞ *Big Sur* by Jack Kerouac: Published after *On the Road* made Kerouac an overnight sensation, this thinly veiled novel portrays a famous writer escaping the pressures of success in the natural beauty of the Central Coast: "Yay, for this, more aloneness."

....

☞ *Where I Was From* by Joan Didion: Three and a half decades after *Slouching Towards Bethlehem* came out, the patron saint of creative nonfiction explores her Sacramento upbringing and bridges the gaps between the state's myths and realities.

LODGING

BAY VIEWS
Nick's Cove
Marshall
nickscove.com
Stilted cottages on misty Tomales Bay, plus a long dock made for oyster devouring.

....

VICTORIAN B&B
Joshua Grindle Inn
Mendocino
joshuagrindlemen docino.com
Charming water tower conversion, one of a few that recall Mendo's heyday.

....

FIRE TOWER
Calpine Lookout
Tahoe National Forest
recreation.gov
Decommissioned observation tower. No water or electricity; views for days.

....

BEACHY '50s
The Surfrider Malibu
Malibu
thesurfridermalibu.com
Classic midcentury motel, boutiquefied for maximum surf-adjacent relaxation.

CLIFFTOP ESCAPE
Post Ranch Inn
Big Sur
postranchinn.com
Bucket list-worthy suites, treehouses perched 1,200 cliffside feet above the Pacific.

....

AIRSTREAMS
AutoCamp
Guerneville
autocamp.com
Glamp among Russian River redwoods; a Yosemite outpost as well.

....

NAPA RESORT
Calistoga Motor Lodge
calistogamotorlodge andspa.com
Chic reinvention of the roadside classic, mineral pools aplenty.

....

RUSTIC RANCH
Drakesbad Guest Ranch
Chester
lassenlodging.com
Secluded lodge at southeast end of Lassen Volcanic National Park.

WELLNESS ENCLAVE
Ojai Valley Inn
Ojai
ojaivalleyinn.com
Sprawling mission-style resort and spa tucked in Topatopa range.

....

RETRO GLAMOUR
Sunset Tower
Los Angeles
sunsettowerhotel.com
Hollywood deals happen at The Tower Bar, where the maître d' is former *Vogue* editor Gabe Doppelt.

....

BEACHSIDE BEAUTE
Hotel Joaquin
Laguna Beach
hoteljoaquin.com
22 rooms tucked into Shaw's Cove; lounge with your nightcap in the "Living Room."

....

MIDCENTURY MODERN
Parker Palm Springs
parkerpalmsprings.com
Gene Autry's baseball team training facility; now colorful Jonathan Adler-decorated retreat.

PARKS AND PUBLIC LANDS

Exemplary entry points into the state's varied landscapes and wilderness.

ANZA-BORREGO DESERT STATE PARK
Sweeping desert vistas surrounded by Vallecito and Santa Rosa mountains to the south and north; carpeted by blooming wildflowers each Spring. *See: Borrego Palm Canyon and Cactus Loop trails*

....

DOHENY STATE BEACH
California's first state beach; 62 acres begging for a rinse and repeat schedule of surfing, dozing and picnicking. Thanks to rocky bottom, consistent 3- to 4-footers make it perfect for beginners. *See: Doheny State Beach campground and trail*

....

KLAMATH NATIONAL FOREST
Jagged peaks, golden valleys and alpine lakes converge in the North's Cascade Range. Permits required for Trinity Alps Wilderness treks. *See: Black Butte Trail, Kangaroo Lake Campground*

....

EMERALD BAY STATE PARK
Lake Tahoe's National Natural Landmark whose trails reveal beauty above and below the waterline; snorkelers able to investigate underwater wreckage. *See: Fannette Island, Eagle Falls trail*

....

HUMBOLDT REDWOODS STATE PARK
Ideal spot to be surrounded by massive sunlight-filtering old growth; 17,000 acres' worth make it world's largest. Stratosphere Giant [park's tallest] location kept secret for protection. *See: Founder's Grove, Julia Morgan's Hearthstone.*

....

JULIA PFEIFFER BURNS & PFEIFFER BIG SUR STATE PARKS
Central Coast's embarrassment of riches has been tagged "mini Yosemite." Big Sur's purple-sand beach is reached via unsigned road, off Hwy 1. *See: Pfeiffer Beach, McWay Fall.*

....

POINT REYES NATIONAL SEASHORE
Spot migrating whales and elephant seals on this pristinely rugged coast, backed by tree-laden ridges and sloping grasslands, just one hour north of San Francisco. *See: Alamere Falls, Tomales Point Trail*

ISSUES

Water	Hotter temperatures and waning rainfall exacerbate droughts as well as floods, while thirsty cities compete with farmers and wildlife for water rights. Existing reservoirs, basins and aqueducts may not match future needs. **EXPERT:** *Jeffrey Mount, Public Policy Institute of California, Water Policy Center*
Housing	A growing population will require 3.5 million new homes by 2025, but labor costs and sclerotic laws have slowed construction to fewer than 100,000 units per year. Currently 150,000 Californians sleep in shelters, constituting 25% of the nation's unhoused. **EXPERT:** *Elizabeth Kneebone, Terner Center for Housing Innovation, UC Berkeley*
Fire	While wildfires are a natural component of California's ecology, climate change, mismanaged forests, aging infrastructure and urban sprawl magnify their size and impact. Three-quarters of California's 20 largest blazes have occurred since 2000. **EXPERT:** *Chris Dicus, president Association for Fire Ecology*
Criminal Justice	Despite reforms in the 125,000-inmate prison system, African-American men remain vastly overrepresented, recidivism rates hover at 50% and California's corrections budget is the nation's largest. **EXPERT:** *Charis E. Kubrin, professor of Criminology, Law and Society, UC Irvine*

STATISTICS

3 .... Golden Gate Bridge cables could circle Earth this many times
17,900% .... San Francisco's growth from 1846 to 1852
14 million .... Pounds of marijuana grown annually across the state
131 .... Daily times "Hotel California" is played on U.S. radio
0 .... Places in the world Instagrammed more than Disneyland
1,893,913 .... Acreage burned during 2018 fire season, highest on record
14,495 .... Mt. Whitney summit, tallest in lower 48

GOLDEN STATE

EST. 1850   MOTTO: *Eureka*

STATE BIRD
CALIFORNIA QUAIL

STATE FLOWER
CALIFORNIA POPPY

STATE GEM
BENITOITE

STATE SONG
"I LOVE YOU, CALIFORNIA"

THE BEAR FLAG

CULTURAL LANDMARKS
Disneyland
Anaheim

Golden Gate Bridge
San Francisco

Salvation Mountain
Calipatria

Griffith Observatory
Los Angeles

Hearst Castle
San Simeon

Santa Monica Pier
Santa Monica

SOUTH COAST

HIKING TRAIL
RAZOR POINT
TORREY PINES STATE RESERVE

FARM STAND
FARMERS MARKETS
SANTA MONICA

CINEMA
FOX BRUIN THEATER
WESTWOOD VILLAGE

SMALL FESTIVAL
Sage & Songbirds Festival
Alpine
chirp.org

CLASSIC RESTAURANT
Neptune's Net
Malibu
neptunesnet.com

LIVE MUSIC
Troubadour
West Hollywood
troubadour.com

SCENIC DRIVE
Pacific Coast Highway
Long Beach to San Diego

SWIMMING HOLE
Cooper Canyon Falls
Pearblossom
San Gabriel Mountains

MEMENTO
Sidewinder robe
blockshoptextiles.com

DESERT

- 🏃 **HIKING TRAIL**
  TAHQUITZ CANYON
  NEAR PALM SPRINGS

- 🛒 **FARM STAND**
  CERTIFIED FARMERS' MARKET
  JOSHUA TREE

- 🎬 **CINEMA**
  SMITH'S RANCH DRIVE-IN
  TWENTYNINE PALMS

SMALL FESTIVAL
Desert X
Coachella Valley
desertx.org

CLASSIC RESTAURANT
Lord Fletcher's
Rancho Mirage
lordfletcher.com

LIVE MUSIC
Pappy + Harriet's
Pioneertown
pappyandharriets.com

SCENIC DRIVE
Hwy 78
Julian to Salton Sea

SWIMMING HOLE
Darwin Falls
Death Valley National Park,
west of Panamint Springs

MEMENTO
Healing crystal
Joshua Tree Rock Shop
joshuatreerockshop.com

CENTRAL COAST

- 🏃 **HIKING TRAIL**
  BLUFF TRAIL
  MONTAÑA DE ORO STATE PARK

- 🛒 **FARM STAND**
  CERTIFIED FARMERS' MARKET
  SANTA BARBARA

- 🎬 **CINEMA**
  FREMONT THEATER
  SAN LUIS OBISPO

SMALL FESTIVAL
Old Spanish Days Fiesta
Santa Barbara
sbfiesta.org

CLASSIC RESTAURANT
Industrial Eats
Buellton
industrialeats.com

LIVE MUSIC
Pozo Saloon
Santa Margarita
pozosaloon.com

SCENIC DRIVE
Up the coast
San Luis Obispo to San Simeon

SWIMMING HOLE
Red Rock Pools
Santa Ynez River
Los Padres National Forest

MEMENTO
Redwood Mist soap
Juniper Ridge
juniperridge.com

CENTRAL VALLEY

HIKING: *Feather Falls, Oroville*   **FARM STAND:** *Soul Food Farm Stand, Vacaville*

....

SMALL FESTIVAL

Oakdale Rodeo
Oakdale
oakdalerodeo.com

CLASSIC RESTAURANT

Wool Growers
Bakersfield
woolgrowers.net

SCENIC DRIVE

Fresno County
Blossom Trail
62-mile loop

MEMENTO

Vintage Levi's
Old Gold
shopoldgold.com

SHASTA CASCADE

HIKING: *Thousand Lakes Wilderness, Burney*   **FARM STAND:** *Old Town Saturday Market, Auburn*

....

SMALL FESTIVAL

Bigfoot Jamboree
Happy Camp
bigfootjamboree.org

CLASSIC RESTAURANT

Dining Car Restaurant
Dunsmuir
rrpark.com

SCENIC DRIVE

Feather River Scenic Byway
Follow North Fork of the
Feather River into Sierras

MEMENTO

Elk hair caddis
The Fly Shop
theflyshop.com

NORTH COAST

HIKING: *Coastal Trail, Klamath*   **FARM STAND:** *Kneeland Glen, Eureka*

....

SMALL FESTIVAL

Oyster Festival
Arcata
arcatamainstreet.com

CLASSIC RESTAURANT

The Marshall Store
Marshall
themarshallstore.com

SCENIC DRIVE

Avenue of the Giants
State Route 254
Humboldt Redwoods

MEMENTO

Humboldt Fog cheese
Cypress Grove
cypressgrovecheese.com

CITIES & TOWNS

Ten communities large
and small that capture the
spirit of California

SAN DIEGO

POPULATION **1,425,976**

SIZE **372.4 SQ MILES**

ELEVATION **62 FT**

SUNSHINE **266 DAYS**

COFFEE:
Bird Rock, Coava, Communal, Enoteca Buona Forchetta

BEST DAY OF THE YEAR:
September 22 [fall begins], peak swells

This balmy curl of coastline is a funny mix, part military town and part laid-back flip-flop town. It was a pair of world's fairs that first put San Diego on the 20th century's map—in particular, its 1,400-acre BALBOA PARK, created to celebrate the Panama Canal's completion. The park's botanical gardens and dazzling Spanish Renaissance architecture make it a jewel of the city. [So, too, does the SAN DIEGO ZOO, founded by the surgeon Harry Wegeforth.] Jonas Salk's discovery of the polio vaccine in the 1950s led the city to gift him a swath of oceanfront in La Jolla to build a first-class research lab "worthy of a visit by Picasso." The result is the SALK INSTITUTE [visitors welcome]. Another doctor, with the last name Seuss, settled here after WWII, and the Monterey cypress believed to have inspired *The Lorax* long stood in ELLEN BROWNING SCRIPPS PARK until toppling in 2019. The park remains an electric-green perch from which to watch migrating whales. Want to carve some tasty wedges? Hit Pacific Beach Surf Shop for lessons [or stay dry and view the board collection at Bird's Surf Shed], then sit harborside at MITCH'S SEAFOOD for catch-of-the-day tacos. Avoid decision fatigue over the city's more than 150 breweries by heading to HAMILTONS TAVERN with rotating taps of local beers.

LOCAL TO KNOW

"Wayfarer Bakery in Bird Rock has the best bread in San Diego. The owner, Crystal, has an ability to make complex sourdough look effortless. A perfect place to hang with friends under the passion fruit trellis."
— CLAUDETTE ZEPEDA, chef

PALM SPRINGS

POPULATION **48,375**

SIZE **94.98 SQ MILES**

ELEVATION **479 FT**

SUNSHINE **269 DAYS**

COFFEE:
Koffi, Ernest, Gré

BEST DAY OF THE YEAR:
*Is a whole week, Modernism Week,
every February*

With pools, palm trees and dry desert air that guarantees good hair, it's hard not to feel hipper, prettier and younger in Palm Springs. It's likely why retirees make up half the Coachella Valley's population; the other half knows how to have a good time. Since the Southern Pacific Railroad hit this aquifer-rich expanse, it's been touted as "America's Winter Playground." Bing Crosby threw some serious bashes at his sprawling RANCHO MIRAGE ESTATE for fellow Golden Age stars. Rumored to be where Marilyn Monroe and JFK began their 1962 affair, it's referred to as the "Tryst House." There are plenty of similar midcentury manses to rent for a hedonistic, pool-centric weekend. Iconic hotels, too: KORAKIA PENSIONE for quiet, kid-free, Mediterranean-style romance; and the Ace for the aforementioned good time. No matter what time you wake up, CHEEKY'S serves breakfast, but early birds get the limited cinnamon rolls. Take an afternoon stroll into MOORTEN BOTANICAL GARDEN's cactarium, a desert dreamscape of spiky, fuzzy, twisting, towering cacti and succulents. From the air, golf courses and tennis courts appear to dominate, but downtown is crammed with contemporary galleries and lots of vintage shops as well. When a $200 tangerine polyester halter dress from The Frippery fits, you'll look the part at MELVYN'S CASABLANCA LOUNGE for live piano and potent nightcaps.

LOCAL TO KNOW

*"A great day off is a hike in the morning and margarita
in the afternoon. We like Tahquitz Canyon, where you can do a
2-mile loop and see a waterfall. Then head to lunch
at El Mirasol, our favorite.*
— CELESTE BRACKLEY, general manager Ace Hotel & Swim Club

VENICE

POPULATION **40,885**

SIZE **3.1 SQ MILES**

ELEVATION **10 FT**

SUNSHINE **252 DAYS**

COFFEE:
Menotti's, Great White, Deus Ex Machina, The Cow's End Cafe

BEST DAY OF THE YEAR:
Abbot Kinney Festival

In 1905, a tobacco millionaire named Abbot Kinney unveiled his dream: 14 miles of swampy beachfront, transformed into the charming destination inspired by the Italy he'd encountered decades earlier. Called "Abbot's Folly" by many, unbelievably the plan was a success until the whole of that beachfront was turned into an oil field. After years of industrial languish, the artist set moved in, lighting a counterculture spark that in turn led to an economic rebound. Paddleboards have now replaced the old gondolas, and the Venice Beach Boardwalk features a mile-long street market with surf shops, tattoo parlors and SMALL WORLD BOOKS, an unexpected oasis tucked among the Speedo-clad muscle men and crystal-draped New Agers. The palm-dotted beach path leads to the VENICE ART WALLS, open to all artists and ever-changing since the '60s. Quarter-century-old skate and board brand ARBOR's flagship is filled with bamboo and recycled-wood cruisers and decks, designed by artists like Zoe Keller. Stroll down Abbot Kinney Boulevard, where BAZAR and GENERAL STORE will leave you pining for global antiques and wabi-sabi pottery, respectively. Brunch on GJELINA's brick-lined patio is one of the toughest reservations in the country, but you could always swing by the LA ISLA BONITA truck for a ceviche tostada while you wait. Come sunset, walk the cotton candy canals and raise a glass, at local watering hole THE BRIG, to Mr. Kinney's grand folly.

> LOCAL TO KNOW
>
> *"Venice has always led with originality. Artists set up shop here. The Dogtown guys, they changed skateboarding. Then Snapchat. Every 10 or 15 years there's a significant creative endeavor that changes things. It's that clash of high and low that makes Venice."*
> — GARRETT LEIGHT, founder GLCO

OJAI

POPULATION **7,582**

SIZE **4.36 SQ MILES**

ELEVATION **745 FT**

SUNSHINE **269 DAYS**

COFFEE:
Beacon, Ojai Coffee Roasters,
Coffee Connection

BEST DAY OF THE YEAR:
Lavender blooms on the last Saturday in June

With its hot springs and rumored energy vortex, Ojai has long drawn artists, spiritual gurus and Angelenos seeking respite. Take your morning coffee on a wander through book nerd heaven: BART'S BOOKS is the biggest outdoor bookstore in the country. Other favorite shops include FIG CURATED LIVING, a tucked-away trove of handcrafted goods, and Summer Camp, a 1950s gas station now offering everything from vintage kilim rugs to cheery pennants to custom framing. For lunch, try the crispy fried-chicken sandwich at outdoor eatery THE NEST. Drive into the Topatopa foothills for a taste of the valley's agricultural history at OJAI OLIVE OIL and a hike; Shelf Road is a relaxed trail through tangerine orchards with sweeping valley views. You'll work up an appetite, and luckily, almost everywhere in town offers farm-to-table dining, including longtime barbecue joint OJAI DEER LODGE. Locals are rooting for newcomer Ojai Rotie, which serves up Lebanese rotisserie platters and fresh bread. Bed down at the Ojai Rancho Inn, a cozy revamped motor lodge, but not before checking out what's going down at its tiny wood-paneled bar, CHIEF'S PEAK, where locals and travelers mingle over beer and wine, a crackling fire warms the cooler nights and the pool is open to guests and non-guests alike.

LOCAL TO KNOW

"I first came here to get away from humans. We have that law where you can't build anything higher than two stories and there's no chains, no highway running through. People tell me that they feel like they're in the middle of nowhere, but they're literally 12 miles from Ventura."
— MARIE PIERRE AGOSTINI, Ojai Valley Trail Riding Company

MONTEREY

POPULATION **28,289**

SIZE **8.4 SQ MILES**

ELEVATION **26 FT**

SUNSHINE **267 DAYS**

COFFEE:
Bright, Water and Leaves,
Alta Bakery and Cafe

BEST DAY OF THE YEAR:
Monterey Jazz Festival

In 1945, Steinbeck called Monterey's CANNERY ROW "a poem, a stink, a grating noise, a quality of light, a tone, a habit, a nostalgia, a dream." The heavily touristed waterfront of today is a far cry from such romantic notions: While a hearty helping of Steinbeck references gesture at its sardine-canning past, souvenir T-shirts and saltwater taffy now dominate. That's OK, the deep appeal of Monterey lies elsewhere—both farther in town and just beyond the sea wall. CARPE DIEM FINE BOOKS, a stone's throw from where Robert Louis Stevenson once stayed, specializes in out-of-print and out-of-the-ordinary books, plus a nice collection of local art and collectibles. RECYCLED RECORDS honors the city's musical heritage [R.I.P., Monterey Pop Festival 1967] with a charmingly crammed and impressively diverse vinyl collection. Dining options around town veer European, so the seasonal Oaxacan dishes at CULTURA are extra welcome—look for the street tacos and the calabacitas. But the essence of Monterey is the bay. Monterey Bay Kayaks will get you out onto the water, and Monterey Bay Whale Watch will acquaint you with the local gray whale, humpback and orca community. Finally, there's the legendary MONTEREY BAY AQUARIUM. Like *Hamilton* and sex, the 3.3-acre complex enjoys the rare condition of deserving all its hype. The kelp forest is eerily beautiful, the sea otters tough not to kidnap. Leave a full day for it.

LOCAL TO KNOW

"My favorite walk is the path all the way to Pacific Grove. It's right along the ocean and you can walk for miles and miles and end up at Asilomar Beach. Monterey Bay is a real hard place to leave once you find yourself here."

— JORDAN CHAMPAGNE, co-owner Happy Girl Kitchen

SAN FRANCISCO

POPULATION **889,360**

SIZE **47 SQ MILES**

ELEVATION **52 FT**

SUNSHINE **160 DAYS**

COFFEE:
Pinhole, Ritual Coffee, Andytown, Sightglass

BEST DAY OF THE YEAR:
July 4; rolling fog in the morning, fireworks in the evening

Here's the thing about San Francisco: It is just so beautiful. Yes it's grappling with grave economic disparity, and it may even run out of water one day, but a walk up TELEGRAPH HILL, Bay Bridge on the horizon, gets you right where you need to be. The true essence of SF isn't in its big cultural moments, of which there have been many [Haight-Ashbury's Beats, gold-seeking forty-niners]. It's the funny little corners where someone interesting has created something weird and good. Arguably silent disco beach sun salutations are weird and good; OUTDOOR YOGA SF has a smattering of offerings. Meanwhile, the Audium has been blowing minds since 1967, in pitch blackness, via 176 speakers, with its trippy sound sculptures. At the CHURCH OF 8 WHEELS, an abandoned 19th-century church has reincarnated as a rollicking roller rink. Time your visit to a singalong at the ornate old CASTRO THEATRE, and your inner Moana will thank you. Google your way to a self-guided, calf-killing stairway walk, one of the best ways to embrace those hills—Bernal Heights has great ones. Take a factory tour of Heath Ceramics, then, walk next door to TARTINE MANUFACTORY for a delicious lunch. If you're still in the Mission at dinnertime, you could wade into the endless debate over which burrito is best, or you could simply head on over to TAQUERIA CANCUN. Finally, indulge in the one tourist cliché that's worth every penny: an ALCATRAZ tour.

LOCAL TO KNOW

"There have been some great jazz albums recorded in the Bay Area, but my favorite is Bobby Hutcherson's San Francisco. *Bobby played vibraphone, and this album done with Harold Land is melodic, haunting and a great soundtrack to a foggy San Francisco night."*

— BEN WINTROUB, Tunnel Records

OAKLAND

POPULATION **429,082**

SIZE **55.8 SQ MILES**

ELEVATION **43 FT**

SUNSHINE **261 DAYS**

COFFEE:
*Red Bay, Coloso, Akat Cafe Kalli,
Farley's East*

BEST DAY OF THE YEAR:
Athletics' opening day

The Bay Area's most lively, complicated, rich, poor, strained, mellow, funky and friendly city packs an unfathomable amount in. A glorious stroll through Redwood Regional Park is somehow just minutes from whatever's playing at the PARAMOUNT THEATER, the ornate old deco concert hall, which is somehow just minutes from the OAKLAND MUSEUM OF CALIFORNIA and one of the best history collections in the state; Friday nights there have become a rollicking tradition, with live music, dancing and food trucks. The nearby LAKE MERRITT BOATING CENTER will get you out on the water, but best is to hoof the 3-mile loop around the lake, where the entire city seems to congregate on warm days. Fortify yourself with sweet potato pie at the IT'S ALL GOOD BAKERY, then ponder history: The Black Panther Party, founded in Oakland in 1966, had its first headquarters within these walls; within two years, its radical Free Breakfast for School Children Program was up and running. Oakland's Ethiopian and Eritrean communities have given the city the best doro wat and fit-fit around; ASMARA and Abesha are favorites. Home of Chicken and Waffles is just that, while Fruitvale's Nyum Bai draws crowds for dishes like kuy teav phnom penh. Later, order a greyhound at the demented jumble of a bar that is Cafe Van Kleef. The TEMESCAL FARMERS' MARKET is bountiful and hopping on Sundays, like the city itself every day.

LOCAL TO KNOW

"De Lauer's has been open since 1907. I get into places free. People know me from here. Oakland's a very open city if you're an open kind of person. The difference between Oaklanders and San Franciscans? Um, I don't really know a lot of San Franciscans."
— EMANUEL LEMMA, manager De Lauer's Super Newsstand

SACRAMENTO DELTA

POPULATION **515,264**

SIZE **1,153 SQ MILES**

ELEVATION **-10 FT**

SUNSHINE **188 DAYS**

COFFEE:
Raul's Striper Café

BEST DAY OF THE YEAR:
Isleton Crawdad Festival

Say the Bay Area's present-day shine leaves you jaded of palate—yearning, let's say, for something saltier. The Sacramento Delta, an hour's drive east of San Francisco, offers a throwback reprieve. A thousand miles of lazy waterways snake through frozen-in-time, sparsely populated levee towns. Locke [pop. 75] is the country's oldest rural Chinatown, built under an agreement with a local landowner by Chinese businessmen forbidden from owning their own land. The ANTIOCH DUNES NATIONAL WILDLIFE REFUGE is home—the only home on earth—to the highly endangered Lange's metalmark butterfly; just dozens remain in existence. The hulking OLD SUGAR MILL, a former beet sugar refinery in Clarksburg, now houses a collection of California wineries and their tasting rooms; a lawn outside awaits picnickers. THE DUTRA MUSEUM OF DREDGING isn't quite the Louvre but offers a memorable window onto how a chunk of the state got made; open by appointment. In Walnut Grove, show up at AL'S PLACE, aka Al the Wop's, with your Harley and your love of tiny, remote dive bars. In Rio Vista, Foster's Bighorn harbors one of the great, weird taxidermy displays [also, cold beer], owing to its founding by a big-game hunter-turned-rumrunner. Mostly, though, the delta is for getting out on the water. Patio boats, kayaks and paddleboards can be rented from SUGAR BARGE RESORT, on Bethel Island, and anglers can pull bluegill, stripers, steelhead and even sturgeon from all over.

LOCAL TO KNOW

"You go back in time here. We call it delta time. All those twists in the river, it's very easy to get lost. You're not in the same world as the rest of the world." — BARBARA DALY, Delta Heartbeat Tours

---

SONOMA

POPULATION **11,248**

SIZE **2.7 SQ MILES**

ELEVATION **85 FT**

SUNSHINE **262 DAYS**

COFFEE:
Barking Dog, Sunflower Caffé

BEST DAY OF THE YEAR:
First Thursday in August;
Sonoma City Party

While fur trading Russians first tried to tame these hills, it's really the Spaniards we have to thank for the Sonoma of today: lazy afternoons spent sipping rosé, briny olives at the ready. In 1824, its Franciscans built Mission San Francisco Solano—California's last—and a vineyard, for sacramental wine, along with it. And while for most the Sonoma designation calls to mind 1,768 square miles of windswept coastline and valleys, the municipality for which the county was named happens to be as perfect a small town as ever was. Call ahead for a tasting at SCRIBE WINERY, an oasis with a hilltop hacienda, once crumbling, now exquisitely redone. Afterward, we suggest overordering, everything from pork tamales to octopus tostadas, at EL MOLINO CENTRAL. Swing by General Vallejo's Victorian—in 1834, he transformed the religious mission into a secular town and spread its vines around the region—before taking in sweeping views at the Sonoma Overlook Trail. This will chart you on just the right course to ultimately land at the town's central plaza, where the SWISS HOTEL bar will help you settle in with the easygoing locals. The luxe MACARTHUR PLACE will deliver on all your aspirational Sonoma visions: rustic beams, creamy textiles and snug courtyards. If, come morning, you want to explore the larger county, we suggest tasting Jordan Winery's rich Cabs, QUIVIRA VINEYARDS' jammy Zins and the famed Pinots at Flowers Vineyards & Winery.

LOCAL TO KNOW

"As a winemaker, I aim to capture place and time in the bottle.
The natural expression of our farm in Sonoma. That salty breeze off
San Pablo Bay, the volcanic ashy soil, long nights and foggy mornings."
— ANDREW MARIANI, vintner Scribe Winery

MENDOCINO

POPULATION **894**

SIZE **7.4 SQ MILES**

ELEVATION **154 FT**

SUNSHINE **189 DAYS**

COFFEE:
GoodLife Café

BEST DAY OF THE YEAR:
Third Saturday in March; spot gray whales from Point Cabrillo

One summer night in 1850, an opium-toting clipper ship slammed into a reef 170 miles north of San Francisco. An expedition was dispatched to salvage the remains, but upon arrival they discovered something far more valuable: miles and miles of towering redwoods. A mill was built in what's now Mendocino, and timbermen came from as far as Maine, hence Main Street's saltbox cottages. Eventually, the timber economy faded, which in turn lured artists like Bill Zacha, who founded the MENDOCINO ART CENTER in the late 1950s. A bohemian counterculture took hold, and 60 years later, the center is a thriving presence. The number of communes has dwindled, but the vibe lives on in artist-owned utopias like SALMON CREEK FARM, which hosts workshops and occasionally rents out its perfect cabin [Cedar #7]. Twenty-five minutes south of town, the century-old HARBOR HOUSE INN draws destination diners to its James Beard-nominated restaurant. The ever-changing menu might include kelp-roasted abalone, wrested off the rocks below. For a watering hole, choose your adventure: dive glory at DICK'S PLACE or Mendocino Hotel's lobby bar, which hits a classic [but haunted!] note. Otherwise, pensive walks at BOWLING BALL BEACH, where boulders dot the sand at low tide, are the Mendo way. Along the wild crags of Point Arena-Stornetta Public Lands, where whales spout in the distance, a gorgeous 1,665-acre swath was made a national monument in 2014.

LOCAL TO KNOW

"Mendocino locals are a breed apart, and even visitors get into the mindset. So we're really lucky—anytime I see a book that makes me go, 'That's weird,' I know I'll have a buyer for it. We get a lot of compliments on our science section: The most oddball, obscure topics sell."
— CHRISTIE OLSON DAY, Gallery Bookshop

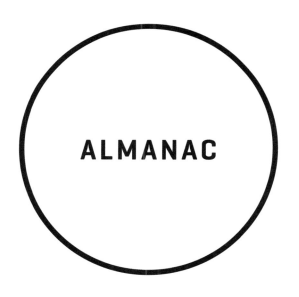

ALMANAC

A deep dive into the cultural heritage
of California through news clippings,
timelines, nomenclature and other
historical hearsay

"GOLD! GOLD!"

Just when we had got partly to work, here came Mr. Marshall with his old wool hat in hand, and stopped within six or eight yards of the saw pit, and exclaimed, "Boys, I have got her now." I jumped from the pit and stepped to him, and on looking in his hat discovered say ten or twelve pieces of small scales of what proved to be gold. I picked up the largest piece, worth about fifty cents, and tested it with my teeth, and as it did not give, I held it aloft and exclaimed, "gold, boys, gold! ... I stepped to the workbench and put it to the second with the hammer. While doing that it occurred to me that while in the Mormon Battalion in Mexico, we came to some timber called manzanita. Our guides and interpreters said that wood was what the Mexicans smelted their gold and silver ores with. It is a hard wood and makes a very hot fire and also lasts a long time. Remembering that we had left a very hot bed of these coals in the fireplace of the cabin, I hurried off and made the third test by placing it upon the point of an old shovel blade, and then inserted it in among the coals ... although it was plated almost as thin as a sheet of notepaper, the heat did not change its appearance in the least. I arose from this third test confident that it was gold. Then running out to the party who were grouped together, made the second proclamation, saying, "gold! Gold!"—*James S. Brown's account of the discovery at Sutter's Mill, January 24, 1848*

GARAGES OF SILICON VALLEY

HEWLETT-PACKARD	APPLE	GOOGLE
367 *Addison Ave* *Palo Alto*	2066 *Crist Dr* *Los Altos*	232 *Santa Margarita Ave* *Menlo Park*
HP began here in 1939 when Dave Packard lived in the first-floor apartment and Bill Hewlett occupied a shed in the back. The co-founders had become friends on a 1934 camping trip.	Steve Jobs was living at his parents' unassuming ranch-style home in the mid-1970s when he and Steve Wozniak built the first Apple computers in their garage.	Larry Page and Sergey Brin were Stanford Ph.D. students when Susan Wojcicki [YouTube CEO] rented her garage to them in 1998. Google's first seven worked here.

THE PONY EXPRESS

On an April afternoon in 1860, a diminutive horseback rider outfitted with a leather mailbag prepared to gallop west from St. Joseph, Missouri. Nobody believed the delivery time this new company promised—10 days to Sacramento—and in a state of disbelief locals gathered to watch history unfold. So exuberant was the crowd that the horse had to be taken away and calmed. Several onlookers plucked souvenir hairs from its tail. California had been a state for only a decade, and the service offered a lifeline to the burgeoning West. At its peak, the company started by William Hepburn Russell, Alexander Majors and William B. Waddell employed 120 riders, with 400 horses distributed at intervals across the route. Riders were small, averaging 135 pounds, and given just two minutes to swap animals. The Pony Express was a miracle of high-speed communication—its crowning achievement was the delivery of President Lincoln's inaugural address, 1,980 miles in seven days and 17 hours—and a financial flop. A year and a half after it began, the transcontinental telegraph put it out of business forever.

PONY EXPRESS OATH

"I, _____, do hereby swear, before the Great and Living God, that during my engagement, and while an employee of Russell, Majors and Waddell, I will, under no circumstances, use profane language, that I will drink no intoxicating liquors, that I will not quarrel or fight with any other employee of the firm, and that in every respect I will conduct myself honestly, be faithful to my duties, and so direct all my acts as to win the confidence of my employers, so help me God."

THE BEAR

The mountains which I have been describing are the favorite haunts of the grizzly bear, the monarch of American beasts, and, in many respects, the most formidable animal in the world to be encountered. In comparison with the lion of Africa and the tiger of Asia, though these may exhibit more activity and bloodthirstiness, the grizzly is not second in courage and excels them in power. Like the regions which he inhabits, there is a vastness in his strength, which makes him a fit companion for the monster trees and giant rocks of the Sierra, and places him, if not the first, at least in the first rank, of all quadripeds. … The grizzly bear of California, in the consciousness of strength and the magnanimity of courage, alone of all animals, stands unappalled in the face of any enemy, and turns not from the sight of man. He may not seek conflict, but he never flies from it. He may not feed upon royal meat, nor feel the flow of royal blood in his veins; but he is unapproachable, overwhelming.

An excerpt from The Adventures of James Capen Adams, Mountaineer and Grizzly Bear Hunter of California, *by Theodore H. Hittell,* 1860

The California grizzly [Ursus arctos californicus] *was hunted to extinction by the* 1920s. *Mountain man James* [*or John*] *Capen Adams is known to posterity as Grizzly Adams.*

THE SOUND BARRIER

Test pilot Chuck Yeager broke Mach 1 [*sea level speed =* 758 *mph*] *above the Mojave on October* 14, 1947. *Almost a year later, Air Force Secretary W. Stuart Symington described the feat.*

The New York Times, Sept. 26, 1948—"Only the other day I was talking to "Chuck" [Capt. Charles E.] Yeager about those flights. … He told of the sun looking clear and sharp like the moon, of stars shining in the black sky … I thought he was going to break into something poetic. 'What were you thinking about?' I asked him. 'I was thinking about how to get down,' he said."

ESALEN

*Stanford grads Michael Murphy and Dick Price founded the
Esalen Institute in 1962. At the forefront of the human poten-
tial movement, the retreat center's mystique endures today:
Mad Men's 2015 finale was based on a facsimile. Below, an
excerpt from its first promotional brochure.*

....

A seminar series exploring recent developments in psychology,
psychical research and work with the "mind-opening" drugs.

A new conception of human nature is emerging in the field of
psychology, a conception that is gradually superseding the views
of classical psychoanalysis and strict behaviourism, a conception
oriented toward health, growth and the exploration of our psychic
potentialities. Creativity research, work with the "mind-opening"
drugs and the discoveries of parapsychology [psychical research]
complement this development, pointing as they do toward a
profounder human possibility. Some scientists and philosophers
believe that this quiet reformulation of psychological thought
will bring the greatest change in the vision of western man since
Copernicus and the Renaissance. It will certainly affect our most basic
attitudes toward human possibility and human destiny.

The charge for each seminar: $16.00 per person per day for single
occupancy, $13.00 for a double [two persons in a room], $12.00 for
a triple. This charge covers room, all meals, use of the mineral baths
and the seminar itself.

> *Esalen's famed hot springs, exclusive to
> institute guests during the day, are open for
> "public night bathing" from 1:00 a.m. to 3:00 a.m.
> Reservations required. esalen.org*

SURFBOARD SHAPERS OF NOTE

SHAPER	DESCRIPTION
David Kawānanakoa *1880s*	*The teenage Hawaiian nobleman carved Santa Cruz redwood into the mainland's first boards.*
George Freeth *1900s-1910s*	*Heroic, Hawai'i-born Redondo Beach lifeguard. Jack London called him "brown Mercury."*
Tom Blake *1920s*	*The founder of California surf culture, hollowed-out vintage Hawaiian designs.*
Meyers Butte *1930s*	*His family-run LA building firm produced the Swastika, the first commercial board.*
Bob Simmons *1940s*	*Adapted naval architecture to board design, still influential. A "mad genius."*
Joe Quigg *1940s-1950s*	*Innovator of hardwood longboards, polyurethane and pintails, outfitted 1940s surfaris.*
Dale Velzy *1950s*	*Postwar materials helped create the nimble "Pig." Credited with first surf shop.*
Hobart Alter *1950s*	*Started in his parents' Laguna Beach pad. Launched a definitive brand.*
George Greenough *1960s*	*Pioneer of fin design key to Nat Young's watershed "Magic Sam" board.*
Bruce Jones *1960s-2010s*	*Hobie vet, credited as the shaper of the modern longboard.*
Cher Pendarvis *1960s-current*	*Surfing mag's first female designer— an expert on handmade boards.*
Jeff Clark *1970s-current*	*Master of Mavericks, titanic NorCal wave. Shapes big guns for huge surf.*
Al Merrick *1980s-current*	*Founder of Channel Islands, go-to for champs and amateurs alike.*
Danny Hess *1990s-current*	*Gorgeous wood creations, true to San Francisco's Outer Sunset scene.*
Ashley Lloyd Thompson *Current*	*A Santa Cruz shaper of aesthetic refinement and sustainability ambition.*

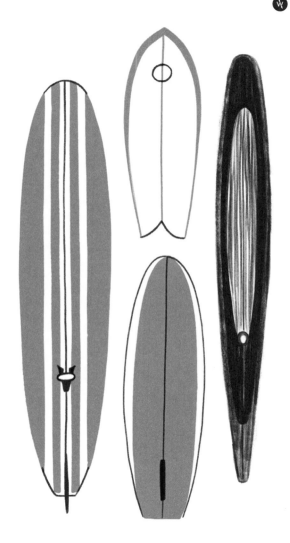

THE FLATLANDS

From 1966 to 1968, The Flatlands newspaper covered a host of issues facing Oakland's African-American population, working under the motto "Tell it like it is and do what is needed." An excerpt from the biweekly's first issue, on March 12, 1966.

Welcome to Oakland, the all-American city; welcome to Oakland, the "city of pain." 380,000 of us people live in this city. Most of the well-to-do whites and a small number of well-to-do Negroes live in the Oakland hills. The nigger-haters and the Uncle Toms and the people that run things, they all live up there too. From their homes they look down onto a patchwork blanket of grey. That's where the flatlands are, stretching out from the base of their hills and running on to the very edge of the bay. The flatlands are spilling over with people. The flatlands stink with decay.

DOROTHEA LANGE

A San Francisco-based studio photographer, Lange shifted her focus during the 1930s and began work as a documentarian for the Relief Administration. In her seminal [and achingly beautiful] "Migrant Mother, Nipomo, California," in which a mother is framed by her worn children, Lange captures the poverty of Depression-era America. Here, Lange recalls the day.

"I saw and approached the hungry and desperate mother, as if drawn by a magnet. I do not remember how I explained my presence or my camera to her, but I do remember she asked me no questions. I made five exposures, working closer and closer from the same direction. I did not ask her name or her history. She told me her age, that she was thirty-two. She said that they had been living on frozen vegetables from the surrounding fields, and birds that the children killed. She had just sold the tires from her car to buy food. There she sat in that lean-to tent with her children huddled around her, and seemed to know that my pictures might help her, and so she helped me. There was a sort of equality about it."

The subject of Lange's 1936 photograph is Florence Owens Thompson. Thompson was unknown until 1978, when reporter Emmett Corrigan located her in Modesto.

CAPITAL CLAIMS

GILROY
Garlic Capital
of the World

GREENFIELD
Broccoli Capital
of the World

ISLETON
Asparagus Capital
of the World

WASCO
Rose Capital
of the World

TULELAKE
Horseradish Capital
of the World

AUBURN
Endurance Capital
of the World

BISHOP
Mule Packer Capital
of the World

BURBANK
Media Capital
of the World

FALLBROOK
Avocado Capital
of the World

CORONA
Lemon Capital
of the World

FORESTVILLE
Poison Oak Capital
of the World

LIVINGSTON
Sweet Potato Capital
of the World

OAKDALE
Cowboy Capital
of the World

SELMA
Raisin Capital
of the World

PALM SPRINGS
Golf Capital
of the World

PEARSONVILLE
Hubcap Capital
of the World

DAVIS
Bicycle Capital
of the World

WILLOW CREEK
Bigfoot Capital
of the World

WATSONVILLE
Strawberry Capital
of the World

VALENCIA
Awesometown

HOME STUDY

KAUFMANN HOUSE
Palm Springs, 1946
In this flat-roofed International Style Richard Neutra home, "horizontal planes resting on horizontal planes hover over transparent walls," according to historian Esther McCoy.

....

GAMBLE HOUSE
Pasadena, 1908
This iconic Arts and Crafts bungalow was built for David Gamble of Procter & Gamble; its Japanese-influenced style emphasizes natural forms.

....

HOLLYHOCK HOUSE
East Hollywood, 1922
A Frank Lloyd Wright home with an abstracted hollyhock-blossom motif, its elaborate split-levels are built around a central courtyard.

....

EAMES HOUSE
Pacific Palisades, 1949
Charles Eames designed and lived in this sleek midcentury modern glass-and-steel structure, considered the most successful of the postwar Case Study Houses.

....

STAHL HOUSE
Hollywood Hills, 1959
You've seen the famed photo of Pierre Koenig's glass box, aglow above L.A. But have you seen it in *Nurse Betty*?

....

SAUSALITO HOUSEBOATS
San Francisco, c. 1960
In five docks, 245 float across from the Golden Gate Bridge. Writer Shel Silverstein called one home.

....

CONDOMINIUM 1
Sonoma County, 1965
Inspired by farm buildings, the Sea Ranch development's timber-framed first unit has single-pitched roofs, redwood siding and Pacific views.

SEEDS

Known as the "Flower Wizard of California," Theodosia Burr Shepherd
was a botanist who built the foundation for the state's seed industry.
Here, highlights from her 1891 catalog.

GIANT OF BATTLES Brilliant crimson, large, very double and sweet. Esteemed one of the finest. *Price 35 cents.*

METEOR A rich, dark velvety crimson Hybrid Tea; a free-bloomer and vigorous grower. *Price 25 to 60 cents.*

MRS. ALPHEUS HARDY The celebrated Chrysanthemum for which $1500 was paid by the introducers. Large, pure white, petals covered with silky hair, giving it a lovely fluffy appearance; called the white ostrich plume chrysanthemum: strong plants. *Price 50 cents.*

THE ARISTOCRAT A most beautiful single variety; immense trusses of a deep velvety cherry color; flowers very large. This geranium is said to have been stolen from the garden of an English nobleman and brought to Santa Barbara. Genuine name not known. To see it, is to desire it. *Ready in April at 25 cents.*

PILOCEREUS SENILIS, OR OLD MAN CACTUS This curious Cactus attracts the attention of every one; it is most grotesque and peculiar, resembling exactly the top of an old man's head [in miniature] covered with white hair. From Mexico. *Price 75 cents to $1 each. Ready April 1.*

ALLIGATOR PEAR

A tree of the tropical species alligator pear or avocado [*Laurus persea*] is flourishing in the grounds of Mrs. F. Sawyer, of Montecito. It was planted by Mr. Silas Bond sixteen years ago, and has borne fruit for the past three years, which has appeared at our horticultural exhibitions. This tree is now about twenty feet in height, and appears in a thriving condition. The bark is smooth; leaves oblong, with prominent veins; flowers yellowish-green; fruit purple in color, with the dimensions of a medium-sized pear, but more oval in shape. It contains a kernel inclosed in a soft rind and yellow pulp. The latter has the delicate rich flavor of the peach, yet to most tastes much more grateful.

—*Transactions of the American Horticultural Society, Volume 5,* 1888

✉

LETTER FROM PRISON

Alcatraz California
March 1939

Deputy Warden
Hon: E.J. Miller

Sir:

A letter in behalf of my case since June 25th at 3:45 p.m. O'clock.

On that date, down at the old garage there were an accident happened and in that accident I. Rufe Perseful No. 84, a prisoner of Alcatraz Island did accidentally lose my left hand.

But the circumstances would not let me tell the truth to you. Therefore, I got the blame for cutting my own hand off, which was and were right, but not on purpose. It happened in the queerest of accidents, which if I had at the time or any time, it would have sounded impossible.

That is the reason why I did not tell, and why that I won't tell. But, Sir, I would not have lost my hand for nothing in the world, believe it or not.

The prison guards here which that I have worked for have not mistreated me. But what do they do? Try to bug me. Am I crazy? Why of course I am. Why? Because they said I was. That is, since that I have been here in the hospital. Oh-no, not all the guard attendants or nurses up here have misused me. Some of them have treated me very nice. But others badly mistreated me.

What the "Department of Health" wants is you to keep clean and sanitary. But they won't let me wash my hands and face, or teeth, before meal. Will you please tell me what I can do about it?

Respectfully,
Rufe Persful

....

—Excerpted from *Letters from Alcatraz* by Michael Esslinger

REDWOODS OF NOTE

GENERAL SHERMAN *Sequoia* *National Park*	Largest tree alive, named by a naturalist who served under Civil War general William Tecumseh Sherman.
GENERAL GRANT *Kings Canyon* *National Park*	Second-largest living tree, declared the "Nation's Christmas Tree" by President Calvin Coolidge in 1926.
HYPERION *Redwood* *National Park*	Named for a Greek Titan, the world's tallest known living tree was discovered in 2006. Location kept secret for its protection.
CHANDELIER TREE *Drive-Thru* *Tree Park*	Named for the shape of its branches, among the "tunnel trees" carved out for cars to drive through
LUNA *Humboldt County*	Activist Julia Butterfly Hill lived in this 1,000-year-old tree for over two years to stave off clear-cutting
HOLLOW LOG *Balch Park*	Nineteenth-century soldiers used this 15-foot-wide, naturally hollowed fallen sequoia as a headquarters
CATHEDRAL TREE *Trees of Mystery*	Nine trees growing together in a semicircle around the stump of one huge original tree that has since rotted away
CHRISTMAS TREE *Humboldt Redwoods* *State Park*	Rare albino redwood, or "ghost tree," a genetic inability to produce chlorophyll leaves its needles white

LEXICON

HEARTWOOD .... *The central part of the tree; dead, but does not decay*

FAIRY RING ....*Redwoods surrounding a long dead parent tree; family circle*

BURLS ....*Knobby masses on trunks; store genetic material*

UNDERSTORY ....*Shrub population below old growth; brilliant rhododendron*

EPIPHYTE ....*Plant using another as its host; roots never touch ground*

CAMBIUM ....*Layer between bark and heartwood, growing part of the tree*

VIRGIN FOREST .....*Woodland that has never been logged*

ROBERT F. KENNEDY AND CESAR CHAVEZ

*From a speech given by soon-to-be presidential candidate
Robert F. Kennedy at a rally in support of Cesar Chavez and the United
Farm Workers in Delano on March 10, 1968. Six days later Kennedy
announced his presidential candidacy. Not even three months later, on
June 5, Kennedy was assassinated at the Ambassador Hotel. He had just
won the California primary.*

The world must know, from this time forward, that the migrant farm worker, the Mexican American, is coming into his own rights. You are winning a special kind of citizenship: No one is doing it for you—you are winning it yourselves—and therefore no one can ever take it away. And when your children and grandchildren take their place in America—going to high school, and college, and taking good jobs at good pay—when you look at them, you will say, "I did this. I was there, at the point of difficulty and danger." And though you may be old and bent from many years of labor, no man will stand taller than you when you say, "I marched with Cesar."

THE CALIFORNIA EAGLE

*In 1879 John J. Neimore founded what would become the California Eagle.
The African American LA-based paper was the first of its kind in the West,
remaining influential until its 1964 closure. Below, an excerpt from the
weekly's April 8, 1916 "Watts Citizens Will," front page story.*

In nearly every political campaign since the birth of Watts the colored voters seem to have been able to get together on issues, and have voted solidly. This spirit on the part of our people points toward a solid successful future for those of us who are turning our faces towards the little city of prosperity ... On next Monday avail yourselves of the opportunity of every good citizen—go to the polls and vote this ticket that your own representative citizens published in this paper because they believe, out of their past experiences that these men if put in office will deal justly with all men. Editor J.B. Bass in company with our San Francisco representative, Mr. H. Shannon, is visiting San Diego and Imperial this week. All along the line Editor Bass is boosting for a bigger and better California for blacks and whites alike.

LGBTQ HISTORY

1700s	Missionaries discover local tribes allow same-sex relationships, cross-dressing.
1850s	With few women in gold fields, men often dance together. Those willing to assume female roles tie kerchiefs around their arms.
1903	Charles Warren Stoddard publishes first relatively open homosexual novel, *For the Pleasure of His Company.*
1947	Under the name Lisa Ben, Edythe Eyde publishes *Vice Versa*, the first homosexual magazine in the U.S.
1950	The Mattachine Society, an early gay rights group, holds first meeting in Los Angeles home of Harry Hay.
1953	First widely distributed gay periodical *ONE Magazine* premieres, Supreme Court finds in favor of mag in subsequent obscenity trial.
1953	Civil rights activist Bayard Rustin arrested for having sex with a man, forced to register as sex offender after serving jail time. Gov. Gavin Newsom posthumously pardons Rustin in 2020.
1954	Atascadero State Hospital opens as hospital for criminally insane, though it eventually becomes known as "Dachau for queers."
1955	Daughters of Bilitis is founded in San Francisco as alternative to lesbian bars, and the country's first national lesbian organization.
1959	Gay patrons fight back against police harassment resulting in LA's Cooper Do-nuts Riot.
1966	Transgender woman throws coffee in face of arresting officer at San Francisco's Compton's Cafeteria, violence ensues.
1969	LAPD officers beat Howard Efland to death outside Dover Hotel, a popular cruising location.
1970	Los Angeles holds its first Gay Pride Parade.
1975	Gay Latino Alliance formed in San Francisco.
1978	San Francisco Supervisor Harvey Milk is assassinated.
1983	First-ever outpatient AIDS clinic, Ward 86, opens.
1984	West Hollywood elects a majority openly gay city council.
2008	After California Supreme Court rules same-sex marriage legal, first marriage license for a same-sex couple is issued.
2011	Gay history becomes required teaching in public schools.

RAMONA

Helen Hunt Jackson hoped her 1884 romance novel, Ramona, *about two star-crossed lovers on a California rancho, would garner support for local indigenous communities. Instead, it sparked a massive tourist industry romanticizing the mission system. The* Ramona Pageant *is still performed every April in the town of Hemet. Here, an excerpt from Carey McWilliams' description of the* Ramona craze, from Southern California Country: An Island on the Land, 1946:

As these hordes of winter tourists began to express a lively interest in visiting "Ramona's land," Southern California experienced an immediate change of attitude and, overnight, became passionately Ramona-conscious. Beginning about 1887, a Ramona promotion, of fantastic proportions, began to be organized in the region. Picture postcards, by the tens of thousands, were published showing "the school attended by Ramona," "the original of Ramona," "the place where Ramona was married," and various shots of the "Ramona Country." Since the local chambers of commerce could not, or would not, agree upon the locale of the novel—one school of thought insisted that the Camulos rancho was the scene of the more poignant passages while still another school insisted that the Hacienda Guajome was the authentic locale—it was not long before the scenic postcards depicting the Ramona Country had come to embrace all of Southern California. In the 'eighties, the Southern Pacific tourist and excursion trains regularly stopped at Camulos, so that the wide-eyed Bostonians, guidebooks in hand, might detrain, visit the rancho, and bounce up and down on "the bed in which Ramona slept." Thousands of Ramona baskets, plaques, pincushions, pillows and souvenirs of all sorts were sold in every curio shop in California. Few tourists left the region without having purchased a little replica of the "bells that rang when Ramona was married."

Reprinted with permission from Gibbs Smith.

THE HEARSTS

The 1849 Gold Rush lured a Missouri-based George Hearst out of anonymous farming and mercantile trading [young Hearst had once taught himself mining] and into the gold fields of California. From Golden State prospecting, he rose to rule Western mining, his scores legion and legend. Hearst took silver from Utah's Ophir Mine, gold from stolen Sioux land in the Black Hills. He backed an obscure Montana operation called Anaconda—soon, the richest copper strike on earth. Mining vaulted Hearst into publishing and politics, and he died a senator in '91. William Randolph, son and heir, took the *San Francisco Examiner*'s reins in '87 and parlayed sensational tastes into the nation's most potent news syndicate. With one legendary headline—DESTRUCTION OF THE WAR SHIP MAINE WAS THE WORK OF AN ENEMY— his *New York Journal* helped launch the Spanish-American War and America's age of empire. To this day, the Hearst name hovers above every airport newsstand browser, every casual perusal of the *Cosmo* website. And, of course, William built Hearst Castle on old family land in San Simeon, funding glorious architectural folly and vast collections with the fortune built on ore and ink. Today the castle is open to the public. *hearstcastle.org*

DISASTERS

EARTHQUAKE   *April* 18, 1906

Magnitude 7.9 hits San Francisco. Destroys 80% of the city, kills thousands, leaves 400,000 homeless.

....

OIL SPILL   *January,* 28, 1969

An oil platform in Santa Barbara explodes, causing the third-largest spill in U.S. history; inspires first Earth Day, April 22, 1970.

....

LANDSLIDE   *January* 3, 1982

A quarter-mile stretch of the Santa Cruz Mountains [600,000 dump trucks' worth] tumbles into Love Creek.

....

FIRE   *November* 2018

The Camp Fire becomes the state's deadliest wildfire on record. Finally contained after 17 days.

CRIME WRITERS

ROSS MACDONALD .... "Find the Woman" [1946]
"The blue-white dazzle of sun, sand, and surf was like an arc-furnace ... The tide had turned and was coming in, all the way from Hawaii and beyond, all the way from the shattered islands where bodies lay unburied in the burnt-out caves. The waves came up towards us, fumbling and gnawing at the beach like an immense soft mouth."

DASHIELL HAMMETT ....*The Maltese Falcon* [1930]
"Where Bush Street roofed Stockton before slipping downhill to Chinatown, Spade paid his fare and left the taxicab. San Francisco's night-fog, thin, clammy, and penetrant, blurred the street. A few yards from where Spade had dismissed the taxicab a small group of men stood looking up an alley. Two women stood with a man on the other side of Bush Street, looking at the alley. There were faces at windows."

RAYMOND CHANDLER .... "Finger Man" [1934]
"In twenty minutes, we were in the foothills. We went over a hogback, drifted down a long white concrete ribbon, crossed a bridge, went halfway up the next slope and turned off on a gravel road that disappeared around a shoulder of scrub oak and manzanita. ... A mountain blue jay flashed across the road, zoomed, banked sharply, and fell out of sight like a stone. ... The man in the back seat got out and held the door beside me open. He had a gun in his hand."

For a modern version of
California noir, see Steph Cha's
Your House Will Pay [2019].

THE STATE OF JEFFERSON

You are now entering Jefferson, the 49th State of the Union. Jefferson is now in patriotic rebellion against the states of California and Oregon. This State has seceded from California and Oregon this Thursday, November 27, 1941. ... For the next hundred miles as you drive along Highway 99, you are traveling parallel to the greatest copper belt in the far West, seventy-five miles west of here. The United States government needs this vital mineral. But gross neglect by California and Oregon deprives us of necessary roads to bring out the copper ore. If you don't believe this, drive down the Klamath River highway and see for yourself. Take your chains, shovel and dynamite. Until California and Oregon build a road into the copper country, Jefferson, as a defense-minded State, will be forced to rebel each Thursday and act as a separate State.

State of Jefferson Citizens Committee / Temporary State Capital, Yreka

ROCK AND HAWK

Here is a symbol in which
Many high tragic thoughts
Watch their own eyes.

This gray rock, standing tall
On the headland, where the seawind
Lets no tree grow,

Earthquake-proved, and signatured
By ages of storms: on its peak
A falcon has perched.

I think, here is your emblem
To hang in the future sky;
Not the cross, not the hive,

But this; bright power, dark peace;
Fierce consciousness joined with final
Disinterestedness;

Life with calm death; the falcon's
Realist eyes and act
Married to the massive

Mysticism of stone,
Which failure cannot cast down
Nor success make proud.

—*Robinson Jeffers,* 1887-1961

From The Collected Poetry of Robinson Jeffers, Three Volumes, *edited by Tim Hunt*

RECORD REVIEWS

THE DOORS
MORRISON HOTEL

"'Blue Sunday' and 'Indian Summer' are two more insipidly 'lyrical' pieces crooned in [Jim] Morrison's most saccharine Hoagy Carmichael style."

—*Lester Bangs, Rolling Stone, Apr. 30,* 1970

....

RITCHIE VALENS
"DONNA" B/W "LA BAMBA"

"Ritchie Valens … turns in a beautiful rock-a-ballad performance on 'Donna,' a lovely name tune. Sound and song are terrific. … On the flip, 'La Bamba,' Ritchie belts out a thrilling cha cha number singing only in Spanish."

—*Cash Box, November* 15, 1958

....

SAWEETIE
HIGH MAINTENANCE

"Her witty one-liners are perfect for fly captions, and her cheeky quotables are ready-made for nights when you're feeling yourself or want to boss up on an ex."

—*Briana Younger, Pitchfork, March* 21, 2018

....

X
LOS ANGELES

"Combining raw tempos and abrasive lyrics with sawed-off Chuck Berry guitar lines, the punkest album of the year almost justified the desperate stupidity of the rest of the band's ingrown scene."

—*Robert Christgau, Village Voice, February* 4, 1981

....

THE GRATEFUL DEAD
THE GRATEFUL DEAD

"…[R]olls with a motion so natural that one suspects the musicians have never listened to the Who or the Kinks… they have developed their own kinetic techniques without reference to the masters in the field."

—*Paul Williams, Crawdaddy, July/August* 1967

CHEZ PANISSE

In 1971, Alice Waters' Berkeley, California, bistro, Chez Panisse, not only defined California cuisine, it cultivated a new ethos in American cooking—fresh, local ingredients, simply prepared. Below, an early menu from a Regional Dinner cooked by Chef Jeremiah Tower, just one of the restaurant's many famous alumni.

....

Northern California Regional Dinner

October 7, 1976 $20.00

Spenger's Tomales Bay bluepoint oysters on ice

Cream of fresh corn soup, Mendocino style,
with crayfish butter

Big Sur Garrapata Creek smoked trout steamed over
California bay leaves

Monterey Bay prawns sautéed with garlic, parsley,
and butter

Preserved California grown geese from Sebastopol

Vela dry Monterey Jack cheese from Sonoma

Fresh caramelized figs

Walnuts, almonds, and mountain pears from
the San Francisco Farmers' Market

᷎

Wine offered by the glass $1.50

Schramsberg Cuvée de Gamay 1973

Mount Eden Chardonnay 1973

Beaulieu Cabernet Private Reserve 1970

Ridge Zinfandel, Fiddletown 1974

Mission Del Sol, Harbor Winery 1974

Tawny Port, East Side Winery

THE BLACK PANTHER PARTY

Speech by Bobby Seale, "Free Huey Newton" rally, Oakland, 1968

I got to explain to you also your soul, your needs, your political desires and needs because that is Huey's soul. ... Now, when we first organized the Black Panther Party for Self-Defense, he would say, "Bobby," he says, "we gonna draw up a basic platform" ... Huey says, We want freedom. We want power to determine the destiny of our black community. Number two, we want full employment for our people. Number three, we want housing fit—decent housing, fit for shelter of human beings. Number four, we want all black men to be exempt from military service. Number five [*APPLAUSE*], we want decent education for our black people in our community that teaches us the true nature of this decadent, racist society ... Number six, we want an end to the robbery by the white racist businessmen of black people ... Number seven, we want an immediate end to police brutality and murder of black people. [*APPLAUSE*] Number eight, we want all black men held in county, state, federal jails and prisons to be released, because they have not had a fair trial ... [*APPLAUSE*] We want black people, number nine, when brought to trial to be tried by members of their peers ... And number 10, he would say, "Let's just summarize it. We want housing. We want clothing. We want education. We want justice. And we want peace." [*APPLAUSE*] That is the basic platform, in case you never knew it or not.

Seale [chairman] and Newton [minister of defense] co-founded the Black Panther Party in 1966. Though the party's popular image centered on its embrace of armed community self-defense, it also initiated radical programs of social and mutual aid. In 1967, Newton was jailed for the fatal shooting of a police officer, charges overturned in 1970. The party's course— tumultuous, violent, yet influential—stretched into the early 1980s.

BOOK	DOCUMENTARY	ARCHIVE
Black Against Empire, an in-depth look, by Joshua Bloom and Waldo E. Martin Jr.	*The Black Panthers: Vanguard of the Revolution* [2016], directed by Stanley Nelson Jr.	Digitized issues of *The Black Panther* newspaper can be found on leftist *libcom.org*

MISSIONARY EXPLORERS

THE PACKET *SAN CARLOS* ARRIVES AT SAN DIEGO
April, 1773

On the 30th the flagship anchored in the harbor of San Diego, having spent on the voyage from Cape San Lucas one hundred and ten days. The captain of the *San Antonio*, seeing that the other vessel was not putting out a launch, although it was inside the port, and being fearful of some misfortune, sent out his own launch. The flagship was found to have all its men infected with the plague ... Since the bark [sailing ship with 3, or more, masts] was infected, and those on board were stricken with scurvy, with the exception of the missionary father, the captain and officers, it quickly spread to the crew of the *San Antonio*, so that in a short time nearly all the men were suffering with the disease, from which thirteen of the volunteer soldiers died. Of the crew of the *San Carlos* only five remained alive, and of the packet *San Antonio* only seven were left. Although all of those remaining were infected, it was God's will to preserve the lives of the twelve so that both barks might leave the port.

—Fray Francisco Palóu, O.F.M.,
Historical Memoirs of New California

RESTAURANTS IN FILM

Mel's Drive-In	American Graffiti	1973	San Francisco
The Prince	Chinatown	1974	Los Angeles
Kansas City Barbeque	Top Gun	1986	San Diego
Cicada	Pretty Woman	1990	Los Angeles
Pat & Lorraine's	Reservoir Dogs	1992	Eagle Rock
Tosca Cafe	Basic Instinct	1992	San Francisco
101 Coffee Shop	Swingers	1996	Los Angeles
Musso & Frank	Ocean's Eleven	2001	Hollywood
Vincenzo's Pizza	Drive	2011	Granada Hills
Hitching Post II	Sideways	2004	Santa Ynez Valley
Smoke House	La La Land	2016	Burbank
Kaldi Coffee & Tea	Lady Bird	2017	Pasadena

CULTS OF NOTE

Pillar of Fire	Founder Alma White demanded complete control over her flock. LA's first policewoman, Alice Stebbin Wells, infiltrated in 1911 to find a missing heiress.
Manson Family	California's most notorious cult family lived briefly with Beach Boy Dennis Wilson, who stole a song from Charles Manson and recorded it as a single.
Divine Order of the Royal Arms of the Great Eleven	So-called Blackburn Cult was started in '20s-era LA by a mother and daughter; sacrificed mules and danced naked while awaiting Christ.
Peoples Temple	Jim Jones and his popular movement moved in 1977 from San Francisco to Guyana, where his 900 followers committed mass suicide.
Heaven's Gate	In 1997, 39 members committed suicide in San Diego in order to leave their bodies and travel with a UFO following the Hale-Bopp comet.
I AM Movement	Los Angeles religious group grew to a million members eager to share financial "love offerings."
Children of God	Small group started in a Huntington Beach coffeehouse. Grew to 15,000 members who practiced a Christianity-meets-free-love religion alleged to include child abuse.
Mankind United	Founder Arthur Bell claimed little men in center of the Earth were fighting "Hidden Rulers." Followers surrendered worldly possessions in exchange for utopia: a shortened work week with free housing.
Hua Zang Si	Buddhist sect led by Dorje Chang Buddha III, a Pasadena man wanted for fraud in China and claiming to be Buddha's reincarnation.

Church of Scientology: Before starting his global religion, science fiction writer L. Ron Hubbard worked with occultist Jack Parsons, co-founder of NASA's Jet Propulsion Laboratory.

LITERARY REALISM

JOAN DIDION *The White Album*

Its principal residential street, the Pacific Coast Highway, is quite literally a highway, California 1, which runs from the Mexican border to the Oregon line and brings Greyhound buses and refrigerated produce trucks and sixteen-wheel gasoline tankers hurtling past the front windows of houses frequently bought for over a million dollars. The water off Malibu is neither as clear nor as tropically colored as the water off La Jolla. The beaches at Malibu are neither as white nor as wide as the beach at Carmel. The hills are scrubby and barren, infested with bikers and rattlesnakes, scarred with cuts and old burns and new R.V. parks. For these and other reasons Malibu tends to astonish and disappoint those who have never before seen it, and yet its very name remains, in the imagination of people all over the world, a kind of shorthand for the easy life.

JOHN FANTE *Ask the Dust*

The old folk from Indiana and Iowa and Illinois, from Boston and Kansas City and Des Moines, they sold their homes and their stores, and they came here by train and by automobile to the land of sunshine, to die in the sun, with just enough money to live until the sun killed them … doomed to die in the sun, a few dollars in the bank, enough to subscribe to the *Los Angeles Times*, enough to keep alive the illusion that this was paradise, that their little papier-mâché homes were castles.

JOHN STEINBECK *Tortilla Flat*

Pilon obligingly stood between Big Joe and the little girls who were running about the bonfire. The Portagee brushed the cold damp sand from his legs and put on his pants. They walked side by side along the dark beach toward Monterey, where the lights hung, necklace above necklace against the hill. The sand dunes crouched along the back of the beach like tired hounds, resting; and the waves gently practiced at striking and hissed a little. The night was cold and aloof, and its warm life was withdrawn, so that it was full of bitter warnings to man that he is alone in the world, and alone among his fellows; that he has no comfort owing him from anywhere.

SCREENWRITING

In his book Adventures in the Screen Trade, *legendary writer William Goldman laid down the commandments of cinematic story.*

1. Thou shalt not take the crisis out of the protagonist's hands.

2. Thou shalt not make life easy for the protagonist.

3. Thou shalt not give exposition for exposition's sake.

4. Thou shalt not use false mystery or cheap surprise.

5. Thou shalt respect thy audience.

6. Thou shalt know thy world as God knows this one.

7. Thou shalt not complicate when complexity is better.

8. Thou shalt seek the end of the line, taking characters to the farthest depth of the conflict imaginable with the story's own realm of probability.

9. Thou shalt not write on the nose—put a subtext under every text.

10. Thou shalt rewrite.

MABEL NORMAND

Chances are you know her. She's the panicked ingénue tied to the train tracks who, with just seconds to spare, is pulled to safety. That icon of the silent film era was played by Mabel Normand, a woman used to firsts. During her lifetime [Normand died in 1930 at 38] the actress and comedienne starred in a total of 190 films, is credited with directing at least 14 and, for a time, served as her costar Charlie Chaplin's mentor. The custard pie lob—a slapstick trademark—well, that was a Mabel Normand first, too.

ROAD TRIPS

Soulful experiences that
take travelers all
throughout California

GOLDEN CALIFORNIA
16-DAY

Crashing waves for miles. Bayside towns, somehow rebellious *and* relaxed. Craggy ranges, shielding sequoias. Anywhere else, any one of these would take pride of place. True to gilded myth, California has it all. Partake in all the fabulous clichés [wine! surfing!], but also steer toward flinty northern hamlets, twangy Central Valley, and Lassen's sleeping volcano. Under the mighty Bear Flag, you've got quite a journey ahead.

———

DAY 1

OAKLAND

Journalist Pendarvis Harshaw talks about his native town and favorite spots to unwind.

Oakland is communal, family-oriented. An outpost for the South for decades. Entrepreneurial in spirit, too—it breeds hustlers. I grew up seeing whatever Too Short did, thinking maybe I can do that with books. My love for Oakland is complicated. Everything is political. The population's changing. It's small enough to wrap your hands around, but large enough to have an impact. Ron Dellums said that.

MIDDLE HARBOR SHORELINE PARK

"If it's sunny and the wind isn't blowing yet, you can see the ships coming in, the fog rolling over the hills in the city," says Harshaw of the former naval supply depot.

....

THE SOUND ROOM

Decades-long labor of love for Karen Van Leuven and Robert Bradsby, whose Broadway jazz club first started in their Oakland home.

....

JOAQUIN MILLER PARK

Named for its 19th c. poet-owner, Harshaw describes as "kind of mystical— there's a pyramid up there. A spot where you can see the entire bay."

....

EAST SIDE OF LAKE MERRITT ON A SUNDAY

"I ride my bike over, see who's there, plop down on someone's blanket, start playing Uno. It's a place to socialize, have a picnic, have a drink, bring a book and never read it," recalls the journalist.

WINE COUNTRY

Napa is absolutely worth a visit and so
are the chiller wine regions nearby.

NAPA VALLEY

Take advantage of the scenery with a tasting-and-picnic combo. Choice spots: Chateau Montelena, Rombauer Vineyards and Rutherford Hill Winery. Hike above the valley at Skyline Wilderness Park, where olive and fig trees were planted by former Napa State Hospital patients. Post-hike, throw open your terrace doors and bask in total luxury at Auberge de Soleil.

ANDERSON VALLEY

From Cloverdale to the coast, Hwy 128 winds through a particularly gorgeous stretch. Stop for Pinot Noir at Goldeneye, Riesling at Phillips Hill or Gewürztraminer at Husch Vineyards' old horse barn. Later, revive with some restorative apple-picking at the Philo Apple Farm.

SONOMA COUNTY

Napa's less-fussy viticultural cousin overfloweth. Sip a Pinot under the old rafters at Belden Barns, a family-owned, small-batch winery. Zo Wines, in Healdsburg, offers lodging. Santa Rosa's Balletto Vineyards carved out a baseball diamond amid its vines for Sunday games. And don't forget to raise a glass at Scribe's Hacienda, the perfect day's end.

UKIAH

The mineral hot springs resort has long offered
healing and escape for the Bay Area chic.

Gilbert Ashoff's life changed in 1971, when, on a trip to Paris, he tasted a bottle of Vichy Célestins spring water. "I'd never had bottled mineral water before. I was hooked," he says. Ashoff and his now-wife, Marjorie, spent the next three years sampling every type of mineral water they could get their hands on. In California, they drove to 33 springs before coming across the rare, naturally carbonated hot spring at Ukiah's VICHY SPRINGS RESORT. He bought the property and set about restoring its historic buildings and alkaline, sodium bicarbonate-rich mineral baths, purported to cure all manner of ills. Guests can ask to see the ancient travertine grotto where Mark Twain is pictured sampling the water with a ladle in his white linen suit.

<table>
<tr><td>DAY
4</td><td>THE LOST COAST
Northern California's wildest and most desolate
stretch of coastline.</td></tr>
</table>

SHELTER COVE

The metropolis of the Lost Coast [pop. 809], where the King Range mountains meet the Pacific—and, oddly, a nine-hole golf course [$15 per round], which follows the coast like a covert Pebble Beach. Artists, hardy surfers and third-generation halibut-and-tuna-hauling fishermen mostly comprise this rugged hamlet. Take a bone-cold dip at Cove Beach, then warm up at Gyppo Ale Mill, which has pizza and beer and Beer Yoga, before bedding down at the Tides Inn.

BLACK SANDS BEACH

Three and a half miles of the stuff, pounded relentlessly by heavy surf. "DANGER, LIVES LOST HERE" the sign warns, but it's beautiful and often empty, save for migrating gray whales and the occasional backpacker. Interested in arriving on foot? For $85, Lost Coast Adventure Tours will shuttle you two winding hours north and drop you at the Mattole Trailhead. It's a three-day hike over boulders, along bluffs and through black bear country back to the beach.

PUNTA GORDA LIGHTHOUSE

Park at Mattole Beach Campground, consult a tides chart, then walk 4 miles through black sand, over dunes and past tidepools until you reach your destination. Originally a 19th-century fog station, it became a lighthouse in 1911, after some 10 ships wrecked near its rocky point. Back then, the lighthkeeper had to travel 11 miles on horseback for supplies in town. Today, travel isn't much easier. It's a bumpy road to the trailhead at the campground; all-wheel-drive recommended.

> *Finding the Lost Coast is part of the fun. Follow Hwy 1 to*
> *Garberville. After a series of redwood-lined switchbacks, proceed*
> *on through Rockport, a once-thriving timber town with a dance*
> *hall, movie theater and post office, until the sawmill closed in 1957;*
> *only the old schoolhouse remains. Continue past Leggett, exiting at*
> *Garberville, then on to Shelter Cove.*

EUREKA

DAY 5

Discover a salty harbor town behind the so-called "Redwood Curtain"—hard to get to, easy to love.

Marijuana manufacturing may account for most of the job growth here, but in its bones Eureka is a fishing town. Humboldt Bay's deep natural harbor built this coastal shelter and its splashy Victorians, by making it possible to ship unprecedented amounts of timber downstream, starting in the 1850s. You can peruse the day's catch at a fresh fish stand inside WILD PLANET at the bottom of C Street, at the edge of the downtown historic district, or head to Dock B on placid WOODLEY ISLAND, where Carol Pinto sells Dungeness crab that her husband, Kevin, hauls in from December to July. Sebastian Elrite of Aqua-Rodeo Farms offers oyster farm tours that culminate at his restaurant, HUMBOLDT BAY PROVISIONS, where you can crack open the day's harvest.

Carson Mansion, est. 1886

DAY
6

YREKA

Home to the Gold Rush Days Festival, flinty Yreka, in the state's far North, steps back in time.

Yreka stands as evidence that California was riding the boom-bust tiger long before Silicon Valley. In 1851, prospector Abraham Thompson glimpsed a speckling of gold in the soil while breaking camp along the Siskiyou Trail. A quick shake of the pan confirmed it was a mother lode. Word spread quickly, and within weeks, 2,000 miners swarmed the "richest square mile on earth"; within months, 5,000. Thompson's Dry Diggings—later incorporated as Yreka—became the county seat, and a city with streets, stores and eventually a railroad, followed. Today, the throwback storefronts of West Miner Street evoke halcyon old times: ZEPHYR BOOKS & COFFEE does exactly what the name suggests, stacked deep with local history and used finds. But when the gold stopped panning out, Yreka shrank—and with it, funding for rural infrastructure. Years later, in 2012, insult followed injury: Thieves stole $1.2 million in historic nuggets from the Siskiyou County Courthouse. Through it all, Yreka maintains a strong sense of self: It is the de facto capital of the State of Jefferson, a collection of counties advocating secession from California since the 1940s.

DAY
7

LASSEN

Head south to tiptoe under a sleeping volcano and through some of the state's most beautiful woodland.

Just after midnight on May 22, 1915, in the tiny town of Old Station, Elmer Sorahan woke to an enormous roar. Nearby Lassen Peak had rumbled to life for the first time in recorded history, pouring hot lava boulders, fast-moving earth and volcanic ash down its steep edge. Sorahan ran to alert his neighbors, as an avalanche of logs and mudflow burst down from the mountain. A century later, the star of LASSEN VOLCANIC NATIONAL PARK is now a massive lava dome, eroded by glaciers into a steep, craggy peak. Visitors can ramble past flatulent mudpots, steam and sulphur vents on the 4.2-mile DEVILS KITCHEN TRAIL, or roam the ashy moonscape of the Cinder Cone Volcano. The LOOMIS MUSEUM contains an antique seismograph and photos of the Lassen eruption captured by a local sawmill-operator-turned-hotelier named B.F. Loomis, offering the earliest pictures of a volcano erupting on U.S. soil.

DAY 8

NEVADA CITY

Two Californias coexist in a raucous mountain town that prizes art, good vibes and cultural preservation.

Nevada City's population drifts somewhere north of 3,000, but you'll see twice that number in the fall, when caravans of seasonal "trimmigrants"— young and flush from long, lucrative weeks pruning marijuana buds—fill the narrow sidewalks, bars and eateries of this historic Gold Rush town. Their presence adds to the already funky flavor of places like ELIXART, an herbal drinks lounge with bottomless kava on Fridays, goddess art, crystals and a bitcoin ATM. By day, writers, artists and tech-preneurs commune along wooden tables at CITY COUNCIL coffeehouse. On the weekends, baby strollers, beer and dreadlocks are ubiquitous at THREE FORKS BAKERY & BREWING CO., where portions are generous enough to be worthy of its name. Bay Area types keep moving here [as evidenced by Priuses sharing the streets with mud-caked 4x4s], and it's not hard to see why. Nevada City's entire downtown is on the National Register of Historic Places, and its palpable charm is matched by a palpable kindness; residents are known to top up one another's parking meters.

DAY 9

DEATH VALLEY

Hottest. Driest. Lowest. Death Valley embodies these head-turning superlatives.

North America's lowest point lies in the rain shadow of five mountain ranges, which strip the winds of humidity and create an arid basin landscape that's otherworldly, even when not registering the hottest temperatures on the planet. Paved roads take you to the panoramic ZABRISKIE POINT and the ghost town of RHYOLITE, which boasted a stock exchange and an ice cream parlor before shutting down in 1916. A gravel road leads to the DEVIL'S GOLF COURSE, which got its name from a 1934 guide book that warned, "Only the devil could play golf" on this rocky expanse. Here, corrugated salt formations extend 1,000 feet underground. You'll need a 4x4 to visit RACETRACK PLAYA, where the wind propels "sailing stones" across a dry lake bed. Death Valley is comparable in size to Puerto Rico, so pay attention to distances and your ability to traverse them. There are three gas stations, at Furnace Creek, Stovepipe Wells and Panamint Springs. Don't count on using your cellphone, or even your GPS.

BAKERSFIELD

Central Valley's Country Music Capital of the West
turned the genre electric and eventually cosmic.

WEEDPATCH CAMP

The setting for John Steinbeck's *The Grapes of Wrath*. This camp, built by the Works Progress Administration for migrants searching for farmwork, produced the first twangs of the gritty Bakersfield sound.

....

KERN COUNTY MUSEUM

Bakersfield-born outlaw country legend Merle Haggard grew up in a boxcar his father converted into a "wood-and-stucco jewel box." After the 2015 "Save Hag's Boxcar" campaign, it was restored and moved to the museum.

....

BUCK OWENS' CRYSTAL PALACE

Owens' fiddle- and pedal-steel-fueled country produced hits such as "Act Naturally" and influenced space cowboys like Gram Parsons and Dwight Yoakam. Owens' music hall still hosts weekly dances.

LOS ANGELES

Who says LA wasn't made for walking? Historian
Victoria Bernal picks three downtown strolls.

BROADWAY THEATRE DISTRICT BETWEEN 3RD AND 9TH STREETS

Amble past vintage movie palaces and pop into the 1893 Bradbury Building. Next door is the pocket park dedicated to African American pioneer Biddy Mason. Cross Broadway to the historic Grand Central Market food hall.

....

LITTLE TOKYO

Start at the Japanese American National Museum on 1st Street and the Geffen Contemporary at MOCA next door. After eating sushi or ramen, cross into Japanese Village Plaza for some mochi ice cream at Mikawaya, where it was invented.

....

LA CIVIC CENTER

After an elevator ride to city hall's viewing platform, meander through Grand Park to the Music Center of Los Angeles County. Head south on Grand Avenue for the Broad Museum. Walk downhill to the art deco Central Library and finish with a cocktail at the Biltmore Hotel.

SANTA BARBARA

Writer, photographer and surfer Jen See reveals how best to experience Santa Barbara and its waves.

In Bruce Brown's famous film, surfers dreamed of perfect swells and The Endless Summer. In Santa Barbara, we dream of endless winter. On a January afternoon, the sun hangs low, a light breeze blows and the tide drops. That's when RINCON, the long point break straddling Santa Barbara and Ventura counties, shines. One of the longest rides you'll find in California, the wave is fast and rollercoaster fun. If you can make it all the way, you'll kick out, legs burning, at the end. November to February is the best window. Afterward, head to nearby Carpinteria for organic eats and cupcakes at Crushcakes Café, coffee at LUCKY LLAMA or beers and food at RINCON BREWERY. Or head south to Ventura for the excellent [and vegan] Harvest Cafe. TAQUERIA RINCÓN ALTEÑO is another simple favorite. Because of the Channel Islands off the coast, Santa Barbara does not have great surf in the summer—but lazy waves slide through on occasion. Bring a big board, head to LEADBETTER BEACH near downtown, lounge in the sand and ride a couple mellow ones. Then head to the nearby Funk Zone district for good eats.

SAN LUIS OBISPO

At the legendary Madonna Inn, a pseudo-Swiss Roy G. Biv wonderland, one can't help but revel in the cheerful extravagance. No beige allowed.

Amids the wildfires, contagion fears and a vast housing shortage, a smaller crisis looms in California: the ever-growing tyranny of good taste. From hipster bars to artisanal co-working spaces, an oppressively pleasing style has swept the state, plastering it with reclaimed wood, Edison bulbs and chic uniformity. Fortunately the cure requires just a three-hour drive up from LA: a pilgrimage to the gaudy old Madonna Inn. What started in 1958 with 12 humble rooms along Hwy 1 became, over time, a 110-room shrine to lavish eccentricity and bygone splendiferousness. A waterfall shower. Cool '50s camp. Classic Spanish flair. Harvard Square. Every room enjoys a different style, cranked to 11, such that staying in all 110—the Old Mill, the Wilhelm Tell, the Krazy Dazy and so on—has become its own bucket list for devotees. [Most popular is said to be room 137, the Caveman. Nearly everything is solid rock, and founder Alex Madonna reportedly created it in six hours.] Part Disneyland, part Flintstones and part roadside motel on steroids, the Madonna is charming, in part, because of what it's not. The flamboyantly pink Gold Rush Steak House isn't quite ironic, the dancers spinning across the dance floor each night not quite campy. For all the plush excess, a welcome sincerity dwells at the heart of the place. The pool, the pool bar, the tennis courts, even the legendary pink Champagne cake: These are swell, but they're beside the point. The point is submitting yourself to the sheer imagination on display, and to the version of California that goes out on a limb, snaps the limb, and builds a new limb from velvet and zebra print.

MORRO BAY

Named for Morro Rock, the ancient volcanic plug jutting out its harbor, Morro Bay's beaches, trails and lagoons cut a stunning figure along the Pacific coast. While the rock itself is off-limits in order to protect the peregrine falcons that call it home, the state park's Portola Point Trail offers sweeping views. Paddleboard rentals abound for those who prefer a sea level perspective.

BIG SUR

Nepenthe restaurant has been a bohemian outpost along Hwy 1 for 70 years. Erin Lee Gafill shares the story of her family's hillside homestead.

My grandparents, Bill and Lolly Fassett, bought Nepenthe in 1947 from Rita Hayworth. She and Orson Welles had bought the cabin during a long drive down the coast. My mother, Holly, was one of five kids, and she and my brother Kirk run the restaurant today. I was born on the property, and I've lived on or near Nepenthe for most of my life. My first job was buttering hamburger buns in the kitchen. What you see here now—the big open restaurant on the hillside, those redwood beams, the terrace—was mostly built by two brothers from Big Sur, Frank and Walter Trotter. Their dad, Sam, built the cabin. They were enormous guys and pretty much made Nepenthe by hand. Big Sur has that quality, of making things by hand, of finding your own meaning. Artists, writers, Berkeley professors who've dropped out. But it takes more than a drive to really get Big Sur. Along the winding road through mountains and forest and cliffs, Big Sur gathers in places like Esalen and the River Inn and Nepenthe, little communities within the place. My grandmother Lolly said that this view and this land were too beautiful to keep to themselves. What's so special about Nepenthe is that it is for everyone. It's egalitarian. You come and buy a sandwich and basket of fries and you can anchor down here. It's a picnic in paradise, 800 feet above the Pacific, whales swimming below, birds singing in the oak trees. I've lived in Lolly's house, the original Nepenthe cabin, since 1989, and still, the natural beauty here confronts you. It's an awe and a mystery. I've painted this for 30 years. I've looked at it my whole life. And still, I wait for that moment when the sun breaks over the mountains.

ESSENTIAL BIG SUR

DEETJEN'S BIG SUR INN	HENRY MILLER LIBRARY	THE PHOENIX SHOP
Fireside daily breakfast, 8am-12pm	Truly a Hwy 1 literary sanctuary	Carries full cache of local makers
TIN HOUSE TRAIL	ESALEN INSTITUTE	VENTANA BIG SUR
Six-miler for high-up Big Sur vista	Buy a three-hour healing arts pass	Stop in the Glass House Gallery

SAN JOSE

In the gleaming heart of Silicon Valley sits a creaky relic of another industry, one that had an equally profound impact on the West.

In 1886, Sarah Winchester, heiress to the Winchester rifle fortune, began fixing up an old farmhouse here. As the story goes, a psychic told her that the souls of all those killed by "the gun that won the West" would haunt her unless construction on her home continued indefinitely. So her team of workers hammered away for 36 years, until her death in 1922. The result was a massive, mad, 161-room Victorian labyrinth, with 10,000 windows, 2,000 doors and assorted stairs-to-nowhere features supposedly designed to elude those vexing spirits. The price tag, in today's dollars: $75 million. For Californians, the WINCHESTER MYSTERY HOUSE is a kitschy holdover from a bygone era. Everyone makes a pilgrimage eventually, or means to, despite the tour's supreme hokeyness. That hokeyness bespeaks something larger about the Golden State, a truism rarely presented so clearly or amusingly. This is a part of the country built on myths, on selling stories about the place in order to make the place. The legend behind the mansion was surely manufactured, a bit of old-timey marketing once de rigueur in California's roadside attraction heyday. But that's a feature, not a bug. Modulate your expectations, wince at the ticket prices and surrender to the charms of this funny old monument.

SAN FRANCISCO

Once a bastion of colonial military power, the Presidio now offers rest, relaxation and reflection fit for an odyssey's close.

End with a stop evoking California beginnings: the fortress, founded in 1776, that served Spain, Mexico and the U.S. Reborn as a national park in the Golden Gate's shadow, the Presidio knits Cali past to present, with a high thread count that may now feel welcome. Two fine hotels, Inn at the Presidio and LODGE AT THE PRESIDIO, convert vintage military quarters with understated swagger that could make anyone wish they'd graduated West Point in 1910. Noted hikes, like shore-hugging Batteries to Bluff, lead to California's very edges. March on to the PRESIDIO SOCIAL CLUB, an ex-barracks now upgraded with a superb bar, and raise a glass to the Golden State: as ever, a place made for looking to the far horizon.

THE NORTHERN RAMBLE
6-DAY

Northern California casts its own distinct spell, conjured from open minds and rangy vistas. Free-spirited writers, farmers, protesters and surfers form an alternative America amid staggering beauty here. Sleepy river towns, towering forests and freewheeling campuses mount a mellow but stubborn resistance to the mainstream—a mindset that invites immersion. Weave through 236 miles. See what you find.

1. BERKELEY 2. SANTA CRUZ 3. SAN FRANCISCO 4. BOLINAS 5. POINT REYES 6. RUSSIAN RIVER

<table>
<tr><td>
DAY
1
</td><td>

BERKELEY
Circled up around one of the state's top
universities is a mix of radical thinking,
barefoot ideals and townie charm.
</td></tr>
</table>

TIME	ACTIVITY
9 AM	Bread heaven at THE CHEESE BOARD COLLECTIVE: an espresso and fruit turnover for now; rustic baguette and hunk of cheese to be enjoyed later.
10 AM	Walk down Shattuck Ave to UC Berkeley, the state's first university, where the free speech movement began. Roam by the Campanile [Sather Tower] and thumb-through MOE'S BOOKS for a Robinson Jeffers collection.
1 PM	Only-local ingredient boards might be customary today, but in 1971, Alice Waters and CHEZ PANISSE launched a food revolution. The upstairs café is open for lunch.
4 PM	More beauty at the Berkeley Rose Garden and CODORNICES PARK. Now is the time for that picnic you stashed earlier.
7 PM	Grab a beer at Freehouse [former headquarters for the FSM] and head to 924 GILMAN ST. Pay $2 at the door to become a member of the alt-music space.

SANTA CRUZ
DAY 2

The sleepy Central Coast surf town remains an epicenter of progressive politics, in a mellow sort of way.

"Nuclear Free Zone." With three words Santa Cruz's City Council voted, in 1991, to enshrine the small Central Coast city forever as a bastion of counterculture politics. Government-blue signs declaring the ban went up all around town that year. So did the replacement signs, after the originals were stolen. On it went, a string of thefts that, in turn, bespoke a deeper truth about the place. This funny old leftie surf hamlet has always been both proud of and amused by its counterculture insistence. Today a distinct resistance to mainstream currents persists. Stubborn old record shops and bookstores remain, but the true weirdness centers around the pace of life. Spend a day at NATURAL BRIDGES STATE BEACH or in the misty redwoods just inland and a slowness drapes over you. Even the lively beach boardwalk—California's oldest surviving amusement park—is soothingly old-timey. Nearly three decades after this small coastal city took on the nuclear establishment, the effort to "keep Santa Cruz weird" has been remarkably successful.

SAN FRANCISCO
DAY 3

As Google buses roll through the fog, the city's outsider cred can get lost. Below, three strongholds.

OUTER SUNSET

Fiercely loyal residents identify as separate from the larger city. THE RIPTIDE epitomizes this independently gruff but friendly attitude. It's a beachcomber's honky-tonk with a fireplace for cold Pacific breezes. *riptidesf.com*

....

NORTH BEACH

Beatnik roots begin inside poet-saint Lawrence Ferlinghetti's CITY LIGHTS BOOKSTORE. He's the original publisher of Allen Ginsberg's *Howl and Other Poems*. Buy an armload of books, and flip a coin for drinks at either Gino & Carlo or Specs. *citylights.com*

....

MISSION

SF's most evocative exposure to the power of art happens when face-to-face with murals in the Mission. Start at PRECITA EYES MURALISTS on 24th St. They run guided tours with deep insight into mural history. *precitaeyes.org*

BOLINAS

DAY 4

The funky West Marin burg is famous for
wishing it weren't.

Just south of the Point Reyes National Seashore, across a small lagoon
from Stinson, sits Bolinas, quietly wishing this paragraph were not un-
derway. It was always thus: As soon as the county hung a sign showing the
way to this unincorporated little town, someone would tear it down. To
visit is to slip into another dimension, one where mom and pop stores,
communal values and bare feet are not the exception, but the norm. At
the BOLINAS PEOPLE'S STORE, Community Center or Bolinas Book
Exchange, an alternative to 21st-century capitalism plays out daily. Absent those familiar patterns, stranger currents govern life here. Walks
take unusual detours, conversations take unusual turns and an unusual
cast of characters moves through it all; the scene in front of SMILEY'S,
the town's cozy old bar, would've occupied O. Henry for years. Mostly,
though, Bolinas is gorgeous. Stroll up along the mesa above town, surf the
legendary waves and, at low tide, join the families mucking about on the
mud flats. That temptation to tell all your friends how nice it is? Stifle it.

POINT REYES

DAY 5

The 60 miles between San Francisco and Tomales Bay
can be damn delicious, if you know where to stop.

CHEESE

COWGIRL CREAMERY has been on the California cheese trail for years; their
Mt. Tam and Red Hawk are standouts. Visit Point Reyes Farmstead for its
award winning Bay Blue and to see the happiest cows in America.

OYSTERS

Tomales Bay is a bivalve paradise. Pull off Hwy 1 and wait in line at The Marshall Store, or go ultra-classic with HOG ISLAND OYSTER CO. Charming is
an understatement here, where reservations are clutch. Third up, order the
BBQ oysters at Nick's Cove restaurant, a bayside mahogany bar dream.

SOURDOUGH

Follow inviting wafts on Shoreline Hwy to BRICKMAIDEN BREADS; grab
a pain au gros [salted potato] or the country white sourdough. If you need
starter intel, Brickmaiden's classes rise to the top.

<table>
<tr><td>DAY
6</td><td>

RUSSIAN RIVER
A family of free-spirited towns where floating the river, roaming redwoods and cracking open a cold one come easy.

</td></tr>
</table>

The evolution of Northern California's rural outposts has generally meant fancification in recent years, which makes the faded-resort-town charm of the lower Russian River doubly appealing. Guerneville, Monte Rio, Forestville, Duncans Mills, Jenner: unfussy old river towns like these get harder and harder to find, an affordable canoe rental [BURKE'S CANOE TRIPS] or afternoon beer [STUMPTOWN BREW-ERY] extra welcome. When shiny new enterprises do move in—the area has welcomed some spiffy restaurants and lodging options in recent years [hello, TIMBER COVE and BOON EAT + DRINK]—they slip into the low-key blue-collar vibe without overwhelming it. Yes, you can now find burrata on Main Street. But you'll find it after a day spent floating down the river, bobbing six-pack in tow. Head north from Jenner to hit FORT ROSS [a visit to the 19th-century Russian outpost is fascinating] or not far from Guerneville you would do well to tuck into ARMSTRONG REDWOODS STATE NATURAL RESERVE. Gaze upwards at 805 acres-worth of sequoias and look for the Parson Jones tree, the park's tallest [310 feet]. The 1,400-year-old Colonel Armstrong is named for the lumberman who helped protect these woods back in 1870.

EXPLORE YOSEMITE
NATIONAL PARK

By Daniel Duane

Four hours east of San Francisco, high in the
Sierra Nevada, Yosemite Valley carves a trough 3,000
feet deep in hard white granite. Waterfalls plummet
down glacier-polished cliffs, climbers dangle from ropes
and families swim in the cold, clear Merced River as it
bends lazily through tall-grass meadows. Meanwhile,
hundreds of square miles all around Yosemite Valley
offer needle-point summits in blue mountain sky,
wildflower pastures and white-sand beaches, and the best
food you'll ever eat at a gas station.

FREE SOLO
2018
Elizabeth Chai
Vasarhelyi &
Jimmy Chin

THE YOSEMITE
1912
John Muir's
contemplations on the
"Range of Light"

**MERCED RIVER,
YOSEMITE VALLEY**
1866
Albert
Bierstadt

**DAY
1**

MARIPOSA GROVE Giant sequoias belong in the
same category as the Grand Canyon: tourist attractions so
obvious and old-school that you're inclined to pass, and so
astonishing that passing would be tragic. Also like the Grand Canyon, they're easy to see: Just park in the dusty lot, follow the trail out
of hot sun into shady woods and have the classic experience of seeing
a few really big trees and thinking, *Gee, those really are big trees, but
I'm still not sure I'm feeling what I'm supposed to feel.* Keep walking,
because those weren't giant sequoias. A little farther down the trail,
you'll see trees bigger than anything you've imagined possible. Stop,
stare and let their sheer scale wake up your sense of wonder.

CAMP 4 The world's most famous campground may
also be its least visually impressive: Camp 4, the scruffy
collection of picnic tables and concrete restrooms that served
as base camp for the most important rock climbs in American history,
including the first technical ascents of El Capitan and Half Dome in
the late 1950s. Climbers from all over the planet still make once-in-a-
lifetime pilgrimages here, and even a casual stroll among campsites is
likely to reveal ropes and hardware and filthy, feverish people chattering
in multiple languages about their next adventure on nearby cliffs.

> DAY 2

AHWAHNEE HOTEL

The Ahwahnee Hotel was designed in 1927 to bring well-heeled
visitors back to Yosemite, and the whole grand place epitomizes
a Western-meets-rustic-meets-Native style familiar to those who
have spent time in '20s-era park lodges. The campaign was successful, as the Ahwahnee has hosted everybody from JFK to the
Shah of Iran and even inspired parts of Stanley Kubrick's horror
classic *The Shining*. But the real attraction lies on the back patio,
where bartenders serve El Capitinis—aka the "First Ascent,"
with Smirnoff, Cointreau, pomegranate and other stuff—at
outdoor tables offering the world's finest view of Half Dome.

LEMBERT DOME Stroll from the road onto the
signature feature of the Yosemite high country, rolling
slabs of bulletproof white-and-gold granite. A 2-mile amble
takes you to summit views over vast Tuolumne Meadows, subalpine
greensward and wildflowers on the shores of the Tuolumne River.
Look straight up and imagine the mile-thick ice sheets that buried
everything in sight multiple times over the past 2.5 million years,
carving the entire landscape into its smooth and curvaceous form.

> DAY 3

*At 8,150 feet above sea level, with crystal-clear water under
white-granite domes,* TENAYA LAKE *offers some of the finest
open-water swimming in California.*

DAY
4

MONO LAKE Exiting Yosemite National Park eastbound, Hwy 120 drops fast and steep down the dramatic eastern escarpment of the Sierra Nevada—right into sagebrush on the shores of ancient Mono Lake, thought to have formed at least 760,000 years ago. Freshwater streams flow into Mono Lake but none flow out, so the saline water is too alkaline for fish—but brims with brine shrimp and alkali flies. Two million migratory birds stop here every year, including 35 coastal species that offer the truly strange spectacle of seagull flocks in the high desert. Drop by at sunset, when the atmosphere in the entire basin turns reliably purple, and take in the so-called Tufa Towers, eerie natural limestone formations that resemble abstract sculpture.

> This is going to sound weird, but here goes: You could do a lot worse than carve out a long evening with friends at the Lee Vining Mobil station. The WHOA NELLIE kitchen turns out the best fish tacos and steak Caesar in Yosemite, not to mention barbecued ribs and ahi tuna salad. Warm summer nights often feature live music on lush green lawns where picnic tables look out over Mono Lake.

YOSEMITE CITIES & TOWNS

GROVELAND
Prospectors' town with surly history.
LODGING: Hotel Charlotte
BAR: Iron Door Saloon
GEAR SHOP: Yosemite
Adventure Supplies

FISH CAMP & OAKHURST
Rustic and luxe at park's edge.
LODGING: Chateau du Sureau
BAR: Buffalo Bar
GEAR SHOP: Fish Camp
General Store

LEE VINING & JUNE LAKE
Takeoff zone for lakes, slopes and ghost town.
LODGING: June Lake Pines
BAR: The Antler
GEAR SHOP: Mammoth
Mountaineering Supply

MARIPOSA
A metropolis: pop. more than 2,000.
LODGING: Mariposa Hotel Inn
BAR: Hideout Saloon
GEAR SHOP: Fremont House

MARVEL AT
CALIFORNIA'S TREES

By Heather Smith

In a few days, the dedicated road tripper can bear witness to any number of tree majesty—from the biggest to the oldest, from the fantastical and spiky to absolutely no trees at all. A comprehensive tour would take years, but here's a three-day jaunt to some of the state's most iconic timber, of which John Muir challenged, "If we know a place, we are more likely to protect it."

....

REDWOOD
Sequoia sempervirens
MUIR GROVE
2-mile walk to pristine
old growth

JOSHUA TREE
Yucca brevifolia
LOST HORSE VALLEY
Spanish termed
"Desert Dagger"

MEXICAN FAN PALM
Washingtonia robusta
EXPOSITION PARK
Oldest in
Los Angeles

| DAY 1 | **JOSHUA TREE NATIONAL PARK** Not so much trees as very large yucca shrubs, Joshua trees nonetheless inspire tree-level passions. |

When plant poachers began prospecting east of Los Angeles for ornamental plantings, a Pasadena resident named Minerva Hoyt persuaded Franklin Roosevelt to make Joshua Tree a national monument in 1936 [it became a full-fledged national park in 1994]. Scientists estimate the long droughts that accompany climate change could eliminate Joshua trees from most of the park by 2100, but for the time being, the best Joshua tree spotting is in BLACK ROCK CANYON. In March and April, if there's been enough rain, the trees may be covered in clusters of ravishing and stinky white-green flowers. Those flowers are there for the yucca moth, which crawls out of the ground every spring for an exclusive pollination rendezvous that's been going on for 30 million years or so.

| DAY |
| 2 |

THE PALMS OF LOS ANGELES Not so much trees as very large blades of grass, nonnative palms were planted across LA by the thousands in the 1930s as part of a New Deal jobs program and a boosterish effort to make a semiarid climate look like a tropical paradise. It worked—it's hard to imagine Beverly Hills' CANON DRIVE without the soaring icons. As the palms are attacked by the red palm weevil, the city is replacing them with native trees that shade neighborhoods and filter pollution. As historian Jared Farmer told the *Los Angeles Times*, "The great dying of the palms will be useful to Hollywood too. They love to show how LA is dystopian." For peak palm absorption, head to PALISADES PARK in Santa Monica or Orthopaedic Hospital's PALM DRIVE, where in 187, Charles Longstreet planted the species at his property to welcome visitors.

> DETOUR
>
> *For a look at LA's prehistoric plant inhabitants, as well as the giant sloth that helped distribute the Joshua tree far and wide, visit the La Brea Tar Pits Museum. tarpits.org*

| DAY |
| 3 |

SEQUOIA NATIONAL PARK Sequoias are not only trees, they are *extremely* good at being trees. The largest living creatures on Earth, sequoias live 3,000 years or more and grow up to 300 feet high and 150 feet in diameter. To fully revel in their splendor, we suggest you wake up surrounded: Grab an upstream site at LODGEPOLE CAMPGROUND [book six months in advance, to the day]. The Tokopah Falls trailhead kicks off from here too. A hike along the MORO ROCK and CRESCENT MEADOW TRAIL [more ambitious at 7.3 miles] leads to sweeping views of the Great Western Divide. Prepare to be awestruck.

THE TREE FORMERLY KNOWN AS KARL MARX

The Congress Trail takes you past several of the park's giant-est sequoias, including General Sherman, the world's largest tree. But to the Kaweah colony, a socialist community who built a road into the forest in the 1880s and founded autopian lumber mill, the tree went by the name of Karl Marx. The colony was evicted after the Southern Pacific Railroad, in an effort to protect their own regional lumber and water interests, successfully lobbied for the land to become a national park.

EAT & DRINK YOUR WAY
THROUGH LOS ANGELES

By Gustavo Arellano

Los Angeles has long been a mess of economic disparity, standstill freeways and wave after wave of communities hungry for a slice of it all. Those communities have been making some of the best food in California for decades, even if the culinary establishment doesn't always notice. Work your way through Boyle Heights, Chinatown, Leimert Park and beyond for a window into the city's welcoming food communities.

....

BIG TEN
Beverly Hills Juice
Cold-pressed original
since 1975

MOSCOW MULE
Tam O'Shanter
LA native: Vodka, lime,
ginger beer

ZOMBIE
Tiki-Ti
Cinnamon notes in this
rum-based libation

DAY 1

BOYLE HEIGHTS Jews, Italians, Russians and Japanese all put their mark here, but for the past 50 years, Boyle Heights has mostly functioned as the heart and soul of Latino El Lay. OTOMISAN is the last traditional Japanese restaurant in the neighborhood and a good place to see assimilation in action. A largely Mexican American crowd scarfs down dishes both Japanese American [teriyaki, sushi rolls] and not [oyakodon, a sort of omelet bowl]. Six blocks away is GUISADOS, where suited businessmen wait alongside working-class raza as they queue up for namesake stews and handmade corn tortillas. Duck under I-10 where EASTSIDE LUV's sturdy micheladas fuel the bar's legendary, Mexican-themed karaoke nights—think Juan Gabriel, Selena and, of course, Morrissey.

<table>
<tr><td>DAY
2</td></tr>
</table>

CHINATOWN/OLVERA ST. Modern-day Mexican food arguably began at CIELITO LINDO, a stall on the northern end of Olvera Street open since 1934. Its taquitos are fried-to-order, stuffed with shredded beef and drowned in a creamy avocado salsa that's as much of a city institution as the Dodgers. Here is also Our Lady Queen of Angels Church, where the ongoing immigrant sanctuary movement began in the 1980s. It's a good spot for reflection before you gorge on the sandwiches of the 112-year-old PHILIPPE THE ORIGINAL, French dip heaven, then partake in the Nashville hot chicken variety at HOWLIN' RAY'S, the city's current sandwich du jour. In a city where waiting in line—for a concert, the DMV or in traffic— is a daily ritual, you might as well have a crunchy, hellacious chicken sandwich at the end as a reward. Conclude with snacks at MAJORDŌMO, the first Best Coast outpost of celebrity chef David Chang. The *Ugly Delicious* star changes his menu daily but always lands on bold Asian flavors that make the best of its Cali setting—dried salsa on fried oxtail or avocado on uni.

<table>
<tr><td>DAY
3</td><td></td></tr>
</table>

BALDWIN HILLS/LEIMERT PARK The 3.5-mile Obama Boulevard, renamed for the former president [from Rodeo Rd] in 2019, connects Leimert Park, Crenshaw, Baldwin Village and Baldwin Hills. In this last redoubt of middle-class black Los Angeles, weekend drum circles give way to barbershops and Sunday church. Leimert Park's ESO WON BOOKS is one of the preeminent black bookstores in the country, Roxane Gay cheek-by-jowl with Saeed Jones, Imbolo Mbue and Ta-Nehisi Coates' Black Panther comics. In the same plaza stands the World Stage, where spoken-word nights and jazz sessions happen in between workshops for area and visiting musicians. Swing by ACKEE BAMBOO JAMAICAN CUISINE, a longtime neighborhood favorite that adapts island flavors to its native city. Not only is the namesake ackee served alongside salt fish, but there's spicy chicken quesadillas and a jerk pastrami sandwich that's equal parts Bob Marley and Lower East Side—yet wholly at home in Los Angeles. The farm-to-table soul food of POST & BEAM in Baldwin Hills remains a point of pride for all of black LA. Chef-owner John Cleveland tweaks classics like spaghetti with turkey meatballs and deviled eggs with smoked catfish.

SANTA ANA The OC is not Los Angeles, of course, but an overlooked corner of the city's larger culinary fabric—and Santa Ana is just an hour's light-rail trip from Union Station. Start downtown with LIBROMOBILE, a Latinx bookstore in what used to be a utility closet. Walk to ALTA BAJA MARKET for a great selection of Mexican wines and Southwestern-inspired fare like green chile frittatas and café de olla [cinnamon-laced coffee]. As you walk, keep an eye out for murals that depict everything from Mexican folkloric dancers to the late Kobe Bryant. Take a quick trip to El Centro Cultural de México, which hosts Radio Santa Ana, a low-wattage FM station that hosts news programs and even Mexican death metal hours. Then indulge in Santa Ana's true game: food trucks. From the beef Milanese tacos at ALEBRIJES [known locally as the Pink Taco Truck], to the scintillating Nayarit-style seafood at Mariscos Los Corales, to corn on the cob at Los Reyes Del Elote Asado, the OC's county seat gives LA a run for its lonchera money. Finally, end your day with Peruvian-inflected cocktails at EL MERCADO MODERN CUISINE. There you go—Orange County is actually cool.

INTERVIEWS

Fifteen conversations with locals
of note about family history,
vocational pursuits and the
places they call home

DOLORES HUERTA

CIVIL RIGHTS ACTIVIST

GROWING UP in Stockton trained me. Police would stop and search us because they didn't want to see the white girls hanging out with us.

MY MOTHER STARTED the first Mexican American chamber of commerce. My dad, everywhere he went, would organize a union.

THERE ARE ONLY four or five places on the whole planet where you have the weather you have here in the San Joaquin Valley.

IT ALLOWS US to produce so much of the world's food. And yet we have one of the highest poverty rates in the nation.

WE WERE MEETING with labor leaders and attorneys—Cesar [Chavez] was fasting to protest an Arizona law that prevented farmworkers from striking. They kept saying, "No, no se puede"—meaning, we can't.

I REPLIED, "Sí, se puede. Sí, se puede." I repeated it at the rally later on and it caught on.

I WAS ON the executive board for the UFW. Every time one of the guys made a sexist remark I would put a check in my notes.

AT THE END I'd say, "During the course of the meeting, you guys made 58 sexists remarks." The men were stunned.

IN 1988, we were protesting pesticides in San Francisco. President [H.W.] Bush was staying at a hotel there. We were singing and chanting, then the police moved in.

THE POLICE OFFICER hit me so hard he broke my ribs and my spleen was shattered. I almost died because I was bleeding internally.

I WAS ARRESTED recently with home care workers in Fresno.

WHEN I WAS a little girl, I wanted to be a flamenco dancer. I dance every opportunity I can get.

YES, I'VE BEEN to Burning Man. I love Burning Man.

RON HOWARD

DIRECTOR

I REMEMBER DRIVING from Queens in a '52 Plymouth. Painted Desert, Grand Canyon, over the Mojave Desert and into Los Angeles. I was 4.

WE LIVED IN a tiny one-floor apartment in Burbank.

MY FATHER WAS always writing, memorizing scripts. The most famous thing he wrote was for *The Flintstones*.

WHEN *The Andy Griffith Show* opened, we moved to Hollywood, so we could walk to the studio.

EVENTUALLY THEY BOUGHT a three-bedroom in Burbank. It had a little pool, a big luxury.

MOM AND DAD weren't dazzled by the Hollywood scene.

DAD'S HONESTY AS an actor is what I most admired.

I CHOSE DIRECTING because I loved bearing the responsibility, win or lose. And the director was the person who got to hang out with everybody.

THE PROMISE storytellers make to an audience is that they will be captivated, swept away.

FILMMAKING is logistically awkward.

TOM HANKS IS like Joe DiMaggio. He makes it look so easy, but is wildly intelligent. That combination is remarkable.

I REWATCH *The Graduate* every so often. It's sublime.

MY MOM HAD heart problems, and they knew she was coming to the end, so she asked my dad to go on a car trip to see the redwoods.

I ASKED WHY and she told me, "They are my church."

AND THE CRAZY thing was, when she passed, without knowing about that trip, a friend sent me a note saying, "A redwood has been planted in your mother's name." It was Robin Williams.

DEBBIE WILSON-POTTS

TAVERN OWNER

THE TAVERN WAS built in 1868 by Norman Wines Stagecoach Company. A halfway stop between Santa Barbara and Los Olivos.

WHEN MY GREAT-AUNT passed away, Mom, Dad and I became the owners of Cold Spring Tavern.

WE'RE FAMOUS FOR our tri-tip sandwiches. The guys cook it outside, and they know what they're doing.

MY GREAT-GRANDMOTHER Adelaide and my great-aunt bought the tavern in 1941.

SHE SAW the front door and said, "I'm going to buy that door and whatever comes with it." They lived in the tavern at first.

TRUE mountain women.

THE ONLY THING that we ever worry about is Mother Nature.

I REMEMBER MY great-aunt saying, this Tavern was blessed by an Indian chief and it will never burn down. I hope so.

IN 2007, we had the Zaca Fire. A lot of these firefighters are the same guys that come up on the weekends. They wrapped our tavern up like a baked potato. I've never seen anything like it.

IT WAS A different clientele when I was young—Hells Angels—wild and crazy.

NOW YOU'VE GOT the motorcyclists, CEOs, families, and everybody seems to get along.

PEOPLE COME BACK 30, 40 years later and say this place hasn't changed.

OF COURSE, WE have a lot of stars that come up. We pretend like we don't know who they are.

IT'S IN ARRESTED decay. When it falls down, we just put it back up.

WE DON'T ADVERTISE. The charm of this place is discovering it.

IT'S A LABOR OF LOVE for all of us.

GREGG BOYDSTON

HOTSHOT

I WAS WORKING for Apple and decided to make a change. I loaded up the car and went up to Northern California.

I WAS BOUNCING between campgrounds, waiting for fire calls, hoping to get hired by the Forest Service.

THE INSTRUCTOR SHOWED us a PBS documentary on wildland firefighting, what a hotshot crew does. That got my interest.

IT'S WEIRD 'CAUSE, it is kind of a beautiful thing to see even though it's so destructive.

IT'S LOUD. You can feel heat radiating, there's an ember cast, your eyes, nose are running.

OTHER TIMES, you're two ridges over on a mountaintop and you can't even see the fire.

THE MAJORITY OF the work is creating handline for hundreds of feet, even miles.

IT'S BASICALLY A hiking trail.

You've got a swath of saw cut that removes all the bigger fuel, bushes, branches, trees.

YOUR SUMMER IS gone when you sign up for something like this.

ANYTIME YOU'RE NOT fighting fire you're doing some type of thinning project.

AS TIME GOES on, people live closer and closer to where these things happen.

I'M HERE. ALL my family's here. All the firefighters that are fighting these fires in California are living here.

AT SOME POINT we may need to start thinking about letting fires burn when no one's in danger. It's hard for people to see the benefit.

WE WERE IN Northern California and got a call to head back towards Yosemite. They frown upon helicopters in the park and were talking about looking

for the Mist Trail. That's like a 16-mile hike. We're all laughing, making where's-the-helicopter jokes.

....

ALL GEARED UP, we walked the John Muir Trail as if we're going to summit Half Dome. When we got to the falls, we re-alized the fire was off to the east. At that point they flew us up onto this big granite knob.

....

WE SPENT NINE days up there spiked out—camping, waking up and fighting fires. Eye level with Half Dome.

SOLEIL HO

FOOD CRITIC

FOR MY EARLY life I was raised by my grandparents. We were a working-class refugee family. We didn't eat out a lot.

WHEN I MOVED to New York, my mom cooked when she could, but we ordered out a lot. You got a huge breadth of cuisine.

MCDONALD'S WAS HUGE for us. I still remember the delivery number.

ALICE WATERS' LEGACY is California farm-to-table. Yet in the Chinese restaurants that were here in San Francisco, they were already growing their own produce and poultry.

LOOKING at historical cookbooks, San Francisco's food scene was mostly saloons in the early part of this past century— Hofbraus and chop suey houses.

IN COLLEGE, I'd introduce myself and eventually say, "Yeah, my family's Vietnamese." The response would be, "Oh, I love pho."

ONE OF THE first things I wrote was called "Craving the Other" about cultural appropriation.

I WANTED TO talk about capitalism and environmentalism in a way that didn't alienate anyone.

USING FOOD AS a metaphor was the easiest thing to do. "Why is that burrito more expensive than this one?"

THE CASUALNESS OF crab here in California is so exciting to me. I feel good about eating crab because they would eat me.

YOU CAN GROW anything here. Driving between LA and San Francisco, you see so many almond and pistachio trees.

THAT'S REALLY COOL. I mean, the future's not so cool because you're not going to be able to water those trees.

I EAT OUT six days a week. I have an Instant Pot. It's my best friend.

CHARLES GAINES

ARTIST, PROFESSOR

I MOVED TO California in 1968 for a job at Fresno State.

I WENT INTO this conservative landscape, with these pockets of liberalism, in the university. The polarization made that environment very, very interesting.

AS AN ARTIST, I was still finding myself. I was fascinated by the history of the avant-garde.

A LOT OF artists of color, some friends, began to challenge me. With the general notion that if you're a minority artist then you have the responsibility to make work that addresses racism.

SOME OF THEM accused me of making white art. I thought about it for a lot of years.

I WOULD TEACH people how to think about art critically. There's no reason we need to know how to draw in order to make art. That's a pretty radical thing.

MY WORK is a kind of geometry.

I TRANSLATE THE shape of a tree, from a photograph into a digital image, using numbers written on a grid, and then I use that as a way of overlapping the shape of the same type of object. One right on top of another, in sequence. The later objects don't totally obscure the earlier objects because they're not following the same pathways.

I LIVE IN an area of LA called Cypress Park. When we moved in, it was mostly Hispanic. I liked the fact that it was not a totally white suburb.

THE GANGS IN our area protected us.

THEN GENTRIFICATION happened, and a lot of people moved out, and white people moved in. So right now it's a very, very mixed community.

I LIKE IT because it's so mixed, and it's also become more enriched. I don't have to drive an hour to go to the grocery store.

GENERAL JEFF

COMMUNITY ACTIVIST

I'M BORN AND raised in South Central. I played basketball at Crenshaw High School, and my teammates named me General.

THE FABULOUS FORUM, where the Lakers and Kings played—as a kid I watched both on TV. I've been hooked ever since.

WHEN I WAS five, my mother enrolled me in the Al Gilbert school of performing arts.

A KID DOWN the street had a turntable in his garage. I'd go and swim through the weed smoke to spin the records.

I JOINED UNCLE Jamm's Army. We brought out East Coast rap acts to LA.

I GOT MY first gold and platinum plaque working on Ice Cube's *Lethal Injection* album.

AFTER ALL THOSE years of being a rapper, I didn't want a 9-to-5 job. I did some courier work. I drove a limousine.

FOR THE LAST 13 years, I've been a community activist in Skid Row, the homeless capital of America.

FIFTY CITY BLOCKS. Boundaries created decades ago.

I QUICKLY LEARNED there are three shifts in Skid Row—the day shift, the night shift and the graveyard shift. It's important to have a presence in each.

I LINKED UP with a small handful of residents to start a basketball league and a cleanup campaign, Operation Facelift.

PEOPLE ENCOURAGED ME to join the Downtown Los Angeles Neighborhood Council. I had no idea what that was, but there was a seat on there for Skid Row residents. I won in a landslide.

LA IS THE entertainment capital of the world, also the gang capital of the world.

ALL THIS WORK is like planting a garden.

MIGUEL ORDEÑANA

WILDLIFE BIOLOGIST

I WAS WORKING for the Forest Service, and I'd always wanted to study wildlife in Griffith Park. I grew up right outside it.

IT'S ONE OF the busiest parks in LA, but no one was monitoring it. I put up some cameras, to see if deer and coyotes and bobcats were getting in and out.

ONE DAY IN February, I'm looking at the footage and this massive puma butt crosses my screen. I thought someone must be walking their Great Dane.

I JUMPED OUT of my chair and started fumbling for my phone.

THREE WEEKS LATER he was trapped, given a GPS collar and his blood was taken so they could compare his genetics to other mountain lions they've studied in the past. And they gave him a name, P22. He's the 22nd puma ever studied.

PEOPLE THAT STUDY mountain lions thought it was pretty much impossible. He had to cross the 405, then get to 101. He had to cross Beverly Hills, Bel Air, Studio City.

IT REALLY ALLOWED people from all over the world to see LA differently—not just a place for movie stars and traffic and smog, but a place with amazing biodiversity and amazing species.

LA IS ONE of only two places in the world that has big cats within the city limits. The other is Mumbai.

THROUGH THE REACH of his fame, P22's been able to introduce people to important conservation issues facing urban wildlife.

THERE'S NOTHING WRONG with going to Griffith Park and only playing soccer and having a barbecue.

I WANT PEOPLE to connect with nature, too. I think that opportunity is there more than ever.

BESS KALB

WRITER

I WAS A JOURNALIST, fact-checking for *Wired* magazine. I started writing jokes on Twitter. One day Rob Delaney retweeted one of my tweets. He wrote, "Super funny person alert."

EVENTUALLY I WAS invited to submit a packet to *Kimmel*. I didn't know what a packet was. So I watched 10 episodes and wrote a full episode, from "welcome to the show" to "thanks and have a good night."

I'VE BEEN THERE almost eight years now.

I STILL DON'T consider myself an LA person. There have been times when I've nodded patiently while someone told me about their crystals.

BEING A COMEDY TV writer involves digesting sad news, then processing it into something that makes people laugh.

OVER THE DAY, you're punching up, casting your bit, editing it. If you don't have a bit in that show, you're doing monologue jokes. You're constantly writing.

I'M ABOUT TO release my first book, *Nobody Will Tell You This But Me.* It's my grandmother's life story, and the story of our relationship, told in her voice from beyond the grave.

I STARTED WRITING it the night before her funeral, in 2017. I got up the next day and —this is macabre—I killed.

ONE MORNING IN 2016 the assignment was "Hillary Clinton unveils campaign logo." That night, what people saw on TV was: "Hillary Clinton unveiled her campaign logo today. A lot of people were confused by it but I think it makes perfect sense. The H is for Hillary and the arrow is because she loves archery."

IT TOTALLY BOMBED. It's the joke I'm proudest of. Nobody laughs harder at my jokes than I do.

SACHI CUNNINGHAM

DOCUMENTARY FILMMAKER

I'VE BEEN COVERING big-wave surfing for 20 years.

MAVERICKS IS A big wave in Half Moon Bay. People refer to it as the Mount Everest of surfing. It's one of the biggest waves on the planet, and one of the deadliest.

THE FIRST TIME women surfers asked to compete at Mavericks, they were told they weren't ready. Then the World Surf League said, "We can't afford to pay men and women the same."

THE WOMEN held their ground. The Coastal Commission protected their right to compete through equal access to the coast, and the State Lands Commission said you have to pay men and women equally.

I THINK OF both as very California values.

I'M A THIRD-generation Californian, on the Japanese American side. On May 3, 1942, all persons of Japanese ancestry had 24 hours to gather all their things before being dispersed into camps.

MY GRANDMOTHER WAS three months pregnant. My mom was born inside the barbed wire of the camp and spent the first four years of her life there.

WHEN THE WAR ended, they moved back to Southern California and had to start from scratch.

THIS WHOLE generation my mother's age, they just kept quiet about it and became model minority achievers so that they could blend in.

MORE THAN HALF married white people so that their kids could blend in.

I SEE IT as my duty to remind people of that chapter in history.

I GOT INTO the business of storytelling because of the power that stories can have to create change. Stories like the female big-wave surfers—I don't want them to be forgotten.

LESLIE BERLIN

HISTORIAN

IT STARTED IN the 1950s with eight engineers and scientists who left Shockley [Semiconductor Laboratory], which was started in Mountain View by the inventor of the transistor.

THINK OF transistors like the grain of sand in a pearl. All modern electronics are built around that little bitty transistor.

THEY CAME TO be known as the traitorous eight. They started Fairchild Semiconductor, used venture capital and did it at a time when it was expected you would stay at your employer for 50 years, get your gold watch and retire.

GENERAL COUNSEL FOR their employer told them it was a shameful act and they'd never live it down.

IT WAS ORCHARDS as far as you could see. Beautiful trees that would blossom in the spring.

THERE WAS NO established business culture to push out of the way.

BOB NOYCE, one of the cofounders of Intel, put it this way: "You could shoot an arrow and then draw a bull's-eye around it."

YOU GO FROM farmland to an industrial economy within 20 years. And then very shortly thereafter, it turns almost entirely into a knowledge economy.

UNICORNS are privately held companies valued at $1 billion or more.

STEVE JOBS printed a brochure for Apple in the mid-seventies. In a note, the printer described what he had seen, and at the end he wrote, "Two guys in a garage sounds fishy watch out."

PEOPLE HEAR Silicon Valley and they think of two or three giants. There are thousands of small companies. You definitely can't paint them all with the same brush.

EVERY TIME I drive past the Intel building, I can just picture all those pear trees.

PATRISSE CULLORS

CO-FOUNDER, BLACK LIVES MATTER

I'M BORN AND raised in the San Fernando Valley, in a very working-class, poor community, mostly Mexican immigrants and our black family.

....

A LOT OF policing there, and a lot of overincarceration.

....

MY BROTHER SUFFERED from severe mental illness and ended up in the LA County jail at 19. He was brutally beaten.

....

THAT SHAPED MY understanding of police brutality, my understanding of the use of incarceration.

....

IN 2013, I was living in St. Elmo Village, in Mid-City. It's an artist community founded by Roderick and Rozzell Sykes, an uncle and nephew pair.

....

THEY WERE FINE artists and also activists and gallerists, and they created a home for black creatives.

....

BLACK LIVES MATTER was cre-ated there. Alicia Garza wrote the words and I put a hashtag on it. Those three words meant so much to me.

....

AFTER MIKE BROWN was murdered, we organized a Black Lives Matter freedom ride to St. Louis, with over 600 black folks. We had two goals: to be a support in St. Louis and to come back home and build the movement. And we did.

....

PEOPLE ASK WHERE I'm from and they're like, "Oh, you're a Valley girl." But there's so many different kinds of Valley. I think it's important that people understand how multifaceted Los Angeles is.

....

FOR THE LAST two years, I've been leading the Yes on R campaign, a ballot measure focused on sheriff accountability.

....

I ENVISION AN LA focused on and invested in the most vulnerable, the homeless, the women, the queer and trans folks. That's the LA I'm fighting for.

THAO NGUYEN

MUSICIAN

I WAS TRAPPED in the D.C. suburbs. I always wanted to live in San Francisco. I was like, "It's gotta be even more hills than you see in the opening sequence of *Full House*."

IN 2006, I graduated college, went on my first tour and brought my guitar and giant suitcase.

MY ROOMMATE would be at work scanning Craigslist—I would be at a coffee shop—and she would text my flip phone where we could find a mattress or table.

MY FIRST OPEN mic was at Java House. I remember stopping someone and asking, "Which way to the ocean?"

AT THAT POINT I didn't know I was queer.

I WORKED AT Guitar Center in Virginia so I could afford a Gibson J-45. I still have it.

MY VISION WAS, I would be a touring musician. I just wanted to come home to San Francisco.

THERE WAS NEVER enough time to get a real job. In between tours I would work the farmers markets for Happy Boy Farms.

HEIRLOOM TOMATO SEASON is incredible. I also moved for the fresh produce.

I WAS SCARED. I couldn't say what my life was. Now I can do that more. The last record helped. It was about my dad and our relationship.

THIS IS THE first time—*Temple* is the first record where I could be more specific about my life.

MOLLY IS MY WIFE. I never say that. It's so freeing to say.

SAN FRANCISCO is a landing pad, a hub. So many young queers come to the city trying to find their way and their community.

I WANT TO go backpacking. I fucking love Sports Basement.

EARLONNE WOODS

PODCASTER

WHEN I WAS 17, I committed a crime, went to prison for six years and three months.

I WAS OUT FOR two years, 10 months and went back with a life sentence.

I'M INVOLVED WITH a podcast called *Ear Hustle*. We're a window into life inside prison.

MY SENTENCE was commuted. I was supposed to be in prison until 2028. That's what the three-strike law requested.

A YEAR AGO, I walked out. It's been fast and slow.

INSIDE IT'S QUICK. You look up and your nephew that was just born is 18.

BUT WHEN YOU get out, time is so valuable. A lot of things go slower than expected.

PEOPLE DO CHANGE, people can change, everybody can change.

THE NIGHT THAT I was arrested a light switch went off. You have to do things better.

MY CLOSEST PARTNER was shot five times, died on the scene. He didn't have a weapon. It's what it was. It's what it's always been.

IT WAS JUST a change in my whole perspective of gang shit. I walked away.

I'VE SPENT A total of 27 years in prison. I got to San Quentin for my last seven.

WE BECAME EXPERTS at prisons. We were there 25 hours a day, eight days a week.

WHEN WE STARTED doing the stories, we had an editor and didn't even know how to use the editor. The editor is the seamstress. The person that's going to sew it all together.

THIRTY-SOME STORIES in the can, every story is still hard.

WHEN IT COMES to prisons, you have the prisoner's point of view, the administration's point of view, and then you walk that middle line.

WE STEER CLEAR, for instance, how drugs are smuggled into prison. We're not here to expose you. We just here to tell stories.

IT'S A TRIP when you tell a story where it's almost like back in the day and everybody's gathered around a little speaker and listening to their soap operas.

INSIDE, you don't see the water. You have to find little pockets of windows to see the water.

GETTING OUT was funny. Being able look at the water for a quick second before it was time to get off the property. And I definitely wanted to get off that property.

DID I NEED to be in that prison that long? I would say no.

GETTING OUT and continuing to do the show has been a beautiful thing.

BEING A PERSON that left a lot of people behind in there, it's important because they're like, "If he can do it, I know I can do it." "Hey, man, I need a few dollars on my books." I understand all that shit.

I GO THROUGH my phone and print pictures out. That keeps people pushing forward, to fight hard to get out of prison.

SINCE I'VE BEEN out, I've sat at the table with Governor Gavin Newsom, Secretary Ralph Diaz. Now they're talking to us. It's a difference.

I FEEL A lot of pressure. How you represent as a formerly incarcerated person.

THE NARRATIVE is shifting. And hopefully we continue to play a role in that.

SURVIVORS of crimes, we're hustle.

LOUIE PÉREZ

GUITARIST, SONGWRITER

I GREW UP just east of Boyle Heights, East LA.

MY MOM LISTENED TO Mexican music, and once I was tall enough to change the channel, I found rock and roll.

AFTER SEEING ME play with a toy guitar, she somehow was able to buy me a real guitar.

THE FIRST RECORD I ever saw going around on a turntable was Ray Charles' "Hit the Road Jack."

MY FIRST LIVE music was at the Million Dollar Theatre. The mariachis would start the show with the main singer riding out on horseback.

IF I HADN'T been asked to leave Salesian High School, I would've never met Cesar, Dave or Conrad. We met at Garfield High School, and that was the start of Los Lobos.

WHEN PEOPLE ASK why the longevity of our band—more than 45 years—I say it's because we were friends first, from the same neighborhood.

IN THOSE EARLY days, we played backyard parties, VFW halls and weddings. I always joke that if you were married between 1973 and 1980 and you're Mexican American, we probably played your wedding.

WE STARTED MAKING our own way over the river, where punk music was happening. Chinese restaurants became punk rock clubs after-hours.

WE GOT A deal with a record company, bought a cheap 15-passenger Dodge van and started to tour.

ONE THING WE learned is, don't put out a record in the fall because you end up touring in the wintertime, driving through an Iowa cornfield in the snow.

WHEN WE GOT home, we could hardly wait to have a J&S green burrito.

STORIES

Essays and recollections from
noted Californian voices

HALLOWED GROUND

Written by **GARY KAMIYA** | **BETWEEN AN ALLEY** on one side and a noisy playground on the other, a postage stamp-size piece of ground sits in San Francisco's Mission District, just 40 steps across. It's so small and unprepossessing that most people walk right by. They're missing a magic Narnia door.

This chaotic jumble of often-illegible headstones and grave markers is San Francisco's heart and soul, its deepest place, its historical, spiritual and even metaphysical bull's-eye. And its overlooked quality, its forlornness, is an inextricable part of what makes it so evocative.

Countless losses are memorialized in the Mission Dolores Cemetery, but for me, two stand out: the destruction of the indigenous people and the passing of a never-never land called Yerba Buena. The first was momentous and tragic, while the other was historically insignificant and better mourned with a double shot than a single tear. But between them, the stories of these two losses touch on all four of the city's major epochs—the Ohlone, the Spanish, the Mexican and the American—and they cover pretty much the full spectrum of human existence.

The story of the destruction of the Native people literally begins, and symbolically ends, at Mission Dolores. The squat, whitewashed adobe church, completed in 1791, is the oldest intact building in San Francisco. Its purpose was the same one that drove the entire Spanish colonial enterprise in what was then called Alta California: to save the souls of the Native peoples. The Spanish had good intentions, but their arrival brought mostly misery, disease and death. And it began an inexorable process of cultural extinction that the Mexicans and the Americans were to complete.

At the Mission Dolores Cemetery, this grim harvest is hiding in plain sight. For buried there, and under the surrounding streets, are the unmarked graves of more than 5,000 Indians who died during the

Spanish and Mexican period. This peaceful oasis with its beautiful old trees and tranquil walkways, suffused with an aura of holiness that emanates from the adjoining mission, is simultaneously a kind of Auschwitz—a terrible monument to the most tragic chapter in the city's history.

By comparison, the second of the losses commemorated in the cemetery—the passing of the hamlet of Yerba Buena and the even smaller Spanish-speaking colony near the decaying mission—seems so trivial it's barely worth mentioning. But if the tapestry of a city's history is like a human life, the rollicking, ephemeral and just plain silly are as important as the serious and monumental. Besides, the demise of Yerba Buena is more than a farcical footnote. In its own small way, it is also the story of a paradise lost.

When Spain established Mission Dolores and the 20 other California missions, it was an empire on its last legs. In 1821, Mexico declared independence. Twelve years later, it secularized the missions. Like the others, Mission Dolores quickly fell into ruin. This was catastrophic for the abandoned Indians, but a boon for a handful of former Mexican soldiers and officials. Families bearing names that now grace streets in San Francisco—Sanchez, De Haro, Guerrero, Valencia, Noe, Bernal—acquired vast ranches on former church lands. They also moved into the ruins of the old Mission Dolores complex and built houses nearby. Between 1836 and the early 1840s, these Californios, as they had begun calling themselves, created a little-known, primarily Spanish-speaking neighborhood around Mission Dolores.

At the same time this Californio-dominated quarter sprang up around the collapsing old mission, another community called, Yerba Buena, grew up on the shores of the bay, where the financial district is now. It was populated by a lost-socks-drawer collection of old sea captains, international rovers, eccentrics and drunks. Both places were tiny: In 1846, Yerba Buena and the Dolores colony together had fewer than 300 residents. The two villages, which are usually, if somewhat inaccurately, lumped together as Yerba Buena, were separated by 3 miles of scrub brush and sand dunes, and by cultural and ethnic barriers. But those obstacles did not prevent the Californios and the motley collection of Anglos and other foreigners from mingling. They

befriended one another, drank together, wrestled together, played pool, had eating contests and went on strawberry-picking excursions together. And, in an extraordinary anomaly in 19th-century America, they married one another. In fact, almost all of the prominent Yankee traders in Yerba Buena married Californio women. The editor of the town's first newspaper called Yerba Buena "a half-breed babe—half Mexican and half 'foreign' prodigy."

Somewhat oddly, considering many residents of the hamlet on the cove appear to have spent much of their time completely soused, the Yerba Buena era can be precisely dated. It began on June 25, 1835, when a former seaman named William Richardson erected a lean-to in what is now Chinatown, and ended on January 30, 1847, when the town's name

> **THIS CHAOTIC JUMBLE OF OFTEN-ILLEGIBLE HEADSTONES AND GRAVE MARKERS IS SAN FRANCISCO'S HEART AND SOUL, ITS DEEPEST PLACE.**

was officially changed to San Francisco. Very little actually happened during those 11 years, seven months and five days, which is why I find them the most dreamlike, off- the-wall and lovable period in the city's history.

Yerba Buena vanished without a trace, but Mission Dolores and its cemetery evoke those enchanted years, and the cross-cultural marriages that were their most unusual and endearing feature. One unknown tombstone in particular brings the vanished Yerba Buena era to life more vividly, and poignantly, than any other.

It can be found on the south side of the cemetery, near a stand of Lombardy poplars. The inscription is notable, "In memory of Ann F. Moses, wife of E. Valencia. Born March 3, 1831. Died Feb. 5, 1859." The words appear to commemorate a marriage between a white American woman and a Californio man, virtually unheard of in pre-Gold Rush California. So I looked into it.

One of the few significant events in the short history of Yerba Buena was the arrival in 1846 of the ship *Brooklyn*, whose 239 Mormon passengers doubled the hamlet's population. Twelve-year-old Ann Frances Moses [she was apparently born in 1834, not 1831] and her family were passengers on the *Brooklyn*. The Moses family survived the 24,000-mile journey, but something scandalous and dreadful happened during the voyage. Samuel Brannan, the Mormon Church's representative on the ship, excommunicated Ann's father, Ambrose, as well as a woman named Eagar and two other men, after learning that Eagar and the men had discussed some sort of polyamorous arrangement.

Outcast, the Moses family was not allowed to pitch its tent with the other Mormons near the plaza. Ostracized from Yerba Buena, they headed to the Spanish-speaking colony at Mission Dolores, where her father constructed a lean-to. The Californios were kind to them, giving them all the beef they could eat and telling them where to get water. A young man named Eustaquio Valencia noticed the pretty Ann Frances and began courting her in the traditional Spanish way. Impressed with Valencia, and perhaps feeling that his own diminished status had limited his daughter's marital options, Ambrose Moses gave his approval.

Valencia was from an illustrious Californio family. His great-grandfather José Manuel Valencia came to San Francisco with the Anza expedition; Jose Manuel's wife was the first Spaniard buried in San Francisco, in 1776. Eustaquio's father, Candelario, was married to Paula Sánchez, daughter of the grantee of the vast Buri Buri ranch; Valencia Street is named after him. Eustaquio lived with his family in the Dolores colony.

In 1850, the 16-year-old Ann, who had learned to speak Spanish in the quarter, married the 20-year-old Eustaquio in Mission Dolores. They had two sons, neither of whom lived to adulthood. On February 5, 1859, Ann Moses Valencia died of consumption. She was 24. The widower remarried a Bernal, had 13 children and died in Millbrae at the age of 86.

That unknown tombstone offers a rare, fleeting glimpse of life in the almost forgotten Dolores quarter. The Californio neighborhood near the mission lasted only a little longer than Yerba Buena, its eccentric cousin. As for the Californios, they also faded away. The Yankees overwhelmed them and lawyered them out of their land. Their quasi-feudal culture could not have long survived in the hard-charging new state anyway. But with its disappearance, something simple and gracious in California was lost forever.

That loss, and all the others, are recorded in the Mission Dolores cemetery. The unspeakable tragedy of the Native people. The sad fate of the Californios. The bittersweet passing of the wondrous soap bubble called Yerba Buena. And also recorded are the names of people, famous and unknown, who once lived and died here: Francisco de Haro, Arabella Cora, Jose Bernal, Ann F. Moses. These stories have hallowed this ground. And so those of us who believe, with apologies to Socrates, that the unexamined city is not worth living in, will come here from time to time to ponder, and wonder, and look for fragments that will not crumble in our hands.

GARY KAMIYA is the author of the bestselling book *Cool Gray City of Love: 49 Views of San Francisco* and co-author with artist Paul Madonna of the forthcoming *Spirits of San Francisco: Voyages Through the Unknown City* [Bloomsbury, 2020]. His long-running history column, "Portals of the Past," appears in the *San Francisco Chronicle*. He was a co-founder and longtime executive editor of salon.com.

HERE WE COME

Written by **RACHEL KHONG** | **I WAS 16 WHEN** I first heard the song "California," by the band Phantom Planet. I lived in Southern California, in a suburb 40 minutes from Los Angeles called Diamond Bar, which often smelled of cow shit, because there were rolling brown hills nearby, and cows in those hills, shitting. My family had always lived outside Los Angeles proper: desert towns of desolate strip malls and unnaturally watered, unsuccessful lawns—no beaches or convertibles or sunsets reflecting off ocean water. Mine wasn't the California that people wrote songs about.

At 16, I'd never had a boyfriend. Desperately, I wanted one. I was in love with a boy who, every morning, sat in his red Jeep near my Ford Taurus station wagon, outside our high school, awaiting first period. I don't remember his name and I'm not certain I ever knew it. We never once spoke. One morning, I heard Phantom Planet's "California" playing softly from his car and was spellbound. I bought the CD from my local Target.

Later, "California" became the theme song for a hit television show about high school students living in Orange County, literally 20 minutes—but figuratively a world—away. Phantom Planet consisted of five floppy-haired men-children from Los Angeles, the more-real California. Ostensibly the song was about loving California so much you wanted to come back to it. And sing about it! The chorus, insofar as there was one, was "California, California! Here we come!" The message was exuberant and uncomplicated. Their simple longing for our state struck envy in me. They wanted to come to California, for the simple fact that it was *where they belonged*. I wanted to belong somewhere, though I didn't yet know where.

For them, California was a place to come back to. For me, it was a too-known quantity, and therefore a place to leave.

I headed east for college. Connecticut, here we come! My roommate was from London, and my classmates had grown up in cities like New York and Chicago and Boston—cities that sounded mythical to me, the way California may have sounded to others. Somehow they'd already learned to drink and smoke and make oral arguments in college-style seminars. They owned proper galoshes and knew how to maintain their balance on icy sidewalks. My peers thought they knew what I meant when I said I was *from California*, but whatever picture they had in their mind was a far cry from the truth. Anyway, I was doing imagining of my own: Those kids from New York and Chicago and Boston and the real California—they'd gone to high school house parties like the ones we'd all seen on *The O.C.* And these fellow students from the real California may as well have been older actresses impersonating college students. They Knew Things. I was untenably far behind, and terrified.

What I wanted was to have my own story, stories I imagined my peers already had. Impossibly, I wanted the story to coalesce before I'd even really lived it.

I caught up. I listened to music and attended film screenings and read short-story collections in the library, where everyone else was—and where I should have been—studying. It snowed in Connecticut, so it could have been snowing when I watched the 1994 film *Chungking Express* for the first time. Let's say that it was. It may not have been the first time I heard "California Dreamin'" by the Mamas and the Papas, but it was the first time I really *listened* to it. Here I was in Connecticut, watching a film about people in Hong Kong, listening to a song about California.

Released in 1965 by a quartet of California hippies, "California Dreamin'" is an archetypical song about my state, one of many. California songs are less about a place than the *idea* of a place, even when they're sung by people who've lived here and should know better. Like "California," the premise of "California Dreamin'" is simple: The Mamas and the Papas are in a cold place, longing for the safety and warmth of California.

"California dreamin' on such a winter's day," the Mamas and the Papas sang. While it was true that California was warmer than other places, this was an oversimplified narrative. "I'd be safe and warm [I'd be safe and warm], if I was in LA [if I was in LA]." You wouldn't be safe, necessarily, though it's tempting to believe.

An oversimplified narrative is part of the attraction. Songs aren't written about Oregon or Washington—also beautiful places—at quite the same clip. Maybe California gets all the songs because it's well-endowed, syllable-wise. Maybe it's just that California is ideal for mythologizing. There's the fantasy not only of the place itself, but who you could be in that place: successful, beautiful, carefree. And warm.

What writers of California songs want to believe is that a place can be a shortcut to identity. I had this in common with them. If I could find the context to which I belonged, I thought, I could become whoever I was supposed to be.

I left California, and came back. I left again, came back again. It's possible I listened to Phantom Planet's "California" each time I did. Now I live in San Francisco, a city that tourists visit and songs get written about. According to the songs, San Francisco is a city where you put flowers in your hair and leave your heart. Listen, I get it: It's all eucalyptus trees and unreal blue water and perfect light. Driving, for the hundredth time, over the Golden Gate Bridge, past the bicyclists on their rented bikes, pedaling slowly, still makes me hold breath. Once I'm across the bridge my mind swims again in its minutiae: to-dos, anxieties, all the other human things. Flowers in my hair would never stay put. My heart literally goes where I go.

THERE'S THE STORY YOU SING ABOUT, AND THEN THERE'S THE LIVING OF IT.

It wasn't exactly that I decided I'd live here, I just stopped leaving. I fell in love with a fixer-upper north of San Francisco, near the Sonoma Coast—a little A-frame cabin amid towering redwoods. Buying the house was making a commitment to be here, and this was terrifying to me. I was dating someone I'd dated unsuccessfully twice before and wasn't sure it'd pan out. I wanted to be a writer—I was working on a novel—but unsure I could pull it off. I lacked the clarity I'd always pictured myself, as an adult, having. And the choices I'd longed for, as a teenager, turned out not to be so straightforward, either. One choice meant another life not lived. A choice could be the wrong one. I wondered if I'd made a series of wrong ones.

I tore out drywall and painted cabinets and watched YouTube videos to learn plumbing. I stacked firewood alone and drank wine from plastic takeout containers. I slept sometimes with a chef's knife under my bed, in case I had to stab an intruder in self-defense. In the middle of the night I'd see brown spiders and Google image search what brown recluses looked like, scaring myself awake.

My soundtrack to all this was Joni Mitchell's *Blue* album. I listened to the same side when I was too tired to flip it—always the side with the song "California." In the song, Joni is elsewhere—in Paris, in Greece—and homesick for California. "California, I'm coming home," she sings. "I'm going to see the folks I dig / I'll even kiss a sunset pig / California, I'm coming home."

I've heard Joni was referring to a real pet pig. The pig's owner ran a bar in Malibu, close to where she lived.

There is, to me, a sadness in that song, when Joni sings, "Oh will you take me as I am? Will you take me as I am?" Maybe I hear it because I'm alone—sometimes happy, sometimes lonely—beneath towering ancient redwoods. To me it's about how hard it is to live here because of the beauty. There's a disconnect in the juxtaposition—pathetic fallacy, or mimetic fallacy, or whatever the fallacy is that says that it shouldn't be sunny outside when you're sad, or the other way around: that you shouldn't be sad when a place is this beautiful. Except there is, I suspect, no way around that. There's the story you sing about, and then there's the living of it.

RACHEL KHONG is a novelist living in San Francisco. Her first novel, *Goodbye, Vitamin*, won the 2017 California Book Award for First Fiction and was a *Los Angeles Times* Book Prize finalist. From 2011 to 2016, she was the managing editor, then executive editor, of *Lucky Peach* magazine. In 2018, she founded the Ruby, a work and event space for women and nonbinary writers and artists.

EVER GRATEFUL

Written by **DANA JOHNSON** | **I GREW UP** in the mountains of San Gabriel Valley, in the suburbs of West Covina. Like a lot of children in the '70s and '80s, television was my babysitter. I watched mostly reruns: *Gunsmoke, The Rifleman, Bonanza, The Big Valley, Maverick, The Lone Ranger, The Wild Wild West* and, most of all, *Little House on the Prairie.* I would sit inches away from the screen, enchanted, wanting to be in the frontier worlds I saw. I longed to climb through the set and ride a horse or pump water from a well, pull a gun from my holster and fire. But I was always flummoxed by an incongruity. To watch those shows was inevitably to equate pioneers and cowboys with whiteness.

I placed myself in these vast stretches of land, in the occasional saloon, striking gold as I mined in my calico dress. But in my young mind, I made an exception to the facts in order to accommodate my fantasy. It was like imagining my human self on the moon, except I was the Martian. I learned from these shows that black cowboys didn't exist and neither did black pioneers, not really. When a black person did make an appearance, it struck me as intrusive, like when a little black boy was found hiding in Laura Ingalls Wilder's barn. Laura couldn't believe her eyes, and neither could I. My 12-year-old self found it lacking in verisimilitude.

But of course TV is simply a re-inscription of what white America would have us believe—that the West was won absent any blackness. In fact, African Americans are inextricable from that chapter of history, and from California's origins in particular. They participated in expeditions that lead to the state's discovery, before it had a name. William Alexander Leidesdorff, a biracial businessman, helped found the city that became San Francisco. Enslaved miners brought to California circa 1849—though slavery was illegal—worked and generated the wealth that allowed California to become a viable state. And there were the black men who rode in the Pony Express, closing the gap between the East and West.

Though I would glean none of this from *Bonanza* or *Little House on the Prairie,* it turns out someone had worked tirelessly to bring such contributions to light. Delilah L. Beasley, an autodidactic historian, lifelong newspaper woman and activist, published *The Negro Trail Blazers of California* in 1919. Hers was a mission no one else had undertaken: documenting California's early black pioneers and writing a comprehensive history of black people in the state of California. As groundbreaking as her work was, it was wholly ignored by popular culture. A native Californian myself, I'd never heard of her until relatively recently. I spent a year researching Beasley and came to see that she, like her subjects, was a forgotten pioneer.

Born in 1867 in Ohio, she lost her parents in quick succession as a teenager. She fell in love with California on an early trip here and became part of the African American migration west. She built a jumbled existence here, working variously as a maid, masseuse, manicurist and nurse, even while writing for newspapers. At one point, researching in UC Berkeley's archives for her book, she worked as a cook in the university's archives, "browning the fried potatoes and practicing scalp massage among the students."

Relying largely on the kindness of friends and benefactors, Beasley traveled all over California, interviewing black pioneers and historians. Her queries were often met with disinterest by white interviewees and historians charged with documenting the annals of California. Of course this only reinforced her mission: combating the willful erasure of African Americans' contributions to the West. The pages of *The Negro Trail Blazers* dare readers to refute the facts: *Say there were no Negro pioneers here, no black artists and visionaries, no explorers—my life's work will prove you wrong.* Beasley didn't write like a historian—she wrote like a woman who understood how uninterested white Americans were in African American history. No detail was too small or tangential. She lists trailblazers, name after name, accomplishment after accolade, dating back to one of the expeditions that eventually led to the discovery of California, in 1535. [Apparently, such facts were still contested, so Beasley found someone to translate Spanish documents. "[In] a desire to remove any possible doubt as to the Negro Priest being with Coronado's expedition of exploration in an effort to discover California," she writes, "the writer has been fortunate in having a friend, Miss Buth Masengale, voluntarily to offer to translate some Spanish documents … It seems passing strange that after hundreds of years, a colored girl and a native daughter of California should be the one to translate this document … "]

Beasley includes interviews with people who made epic journeys across the plains, narrowly avoiding massacres by indigenous populations in some cases. She writes of California's first black miner, Waller Jackson, and another, Elige Booth, who described the poor treatment of black miners, adding that "a man was a man, even if he was a colored miner." We learn of Annie Peters, who came to California in 1851 and was the oldest living pioneer of color in 1918. Beasley describes the struggles of Negro pioneers, who sought freedom from racial persecution in the West, often finding it elusive.

Beasley worked through near-death illness and poverty. In a letter to W.E.B. DuBois, she complained that she was tired of her shabby wool coat, whose worn lining she'd restitched many times. She used it as a blanket when she traveled California by train, unable to afford a sleeper car—or a new coat. She literally gave her flesh and blood to the project, suffering a toe amputation after an accident during her travels.

For all that, the book did not sell as she had hoped. Her ambition was to have a copy of *The Negro Trail Blazers of California* in every library in California. Instead, bad reviews and uninterest pushed the volume into obscurity. Except for the academics and scholars who later excavated her life, Beasley suffered the same fate. She died a mostly unknown figure, at the Fairmont Hospital in San Leandro, California, on August 18, 1934. Her tombstone is carved, in somber black marble, with the wrong date of her birth.

Anyone curious to know about California's invisible history can finally find her book, and sift through the names and dates and seemingly incongruous facts for a fuller picture of the West—and of how California came to be. These souls will come to you like apparitions, tapping your shoulder to insist on a place in your memory. One can only imagine what those narratives meant to Beasley, who created a book with such urgent and crowded detail that one reviewer called it a "hodge podge." But she felt she was writing for everyday people, and that she owed it to future generations of African Americans to tell of their struggles. She regarded this not as a burden but a gift, one she was thankful to give. *The Negro Trail Blazers of California* opens with a simple inscription: "Ever grateful. Delilah L. Beasley."

But I am grateful to her, now that I've researched her life as a pioneer in her own right and read about the countless black pioneers who are essential to California's origin story. Why, only in 2019, did I discover her and her stories? While I was staring at my television decades into the future that Beasley imagined—in the very state she wrote about, dismissing the few black pioneers I saw, unable to see myself in these stories—her book was sitting in a library somewhere, obscured, trying to tell me that African Americans were at the center of the story, not the margins. I was not an alien in a landscape that belonged to others, exclusively. I had always been there.

Beasley and I are 100 years apart; she was born in 1867 and I in 1967. I'm a writer from California. I understand her urgency. There are so many stories about African Americans I don't see in the literature, and in California literature particularly. I often wonder: *How will people in the future know who black people were and are, in this place where I was born, this place I claim as mine, that I love as much as Beasley did, if the stories don't tell them?*

This is one.

DANA JOHNSON is the author of the short story collection *In the Not Quite Dark*. She is also the author of *Break Any Woman Down*, winner of the Flannery O'Connor Award for Short Fiction, and the novel *Elsewhere, California*. Born and raised in and around Los Angeles, she is a professor of English at the University of Southern California.

COUNTRY OF LOST BORDERS

[1903]

Written by **MARY HUNTER AUSTIN** | **EAST AWAY** from the Sierras, south from Panamint and Amargosa, east and south many an uncounted mile, is the Country of Lost Borders.

Ute, Paiute, Mojave, and Shoshone inhabit its frontiers, and as far into the heart of it as a man dare go. Not the law, but the land sets the limit. Desert is the name it wears upon the maps, but the Indian's is the better word. Desert is a loose term to indicate land that supports no man; whether the land can be bitted and broken to that purpose is not proven. Void of life it never is, however dry the air and villainous the soil.

This is the nature of that country. There are hills, rounded, blunt, burned, squeezed up out of chaos, chrome and vermilion painted, aspiring to the snowline. Between the hills lie high level-looking plains full of intolerable sun glare, or narrow valleys drowned in a blue haze. The hill surface is streaked with ash drift and black, unweathered lava flows. After rains water accumulates in the hollows of small closed valleys, and, evaporating, leaves hard dry levels of pure desertness that get the local name of dry lakes. Where the mountains are steep and the rains heavy, the pool is never quite dry, but dark and bitter, rimmed about with the efflorescence of alkaline deposits. A thin crust of it lies along the marsh over the vegetating area, which has neither beauty nor freshness. In the broad wastes open to the wind the sand drifts in hummocks about the stubby shrubs, and between them the soil shows saline traces. The sculpture of the hills here is more wind than water work, though the quick storms do sometimes scar them past many a year's redeeming. In all the Western desert edges there are essays in miniature at the famed, terrible Grand Cañon, to which, if you keep on long enough in this country, you will come at last.

Since this is a hill country one expects to find springs, but not to depend upon them; for when found they are often brackish and unwholesome, or maddening, slow dribbles in a thirsty soil. Here you find the hot sink of Death Valley, or high rolling districts where the air has always a tang of frost. Here are the long heavy winds and breathless calms on the tilted mesas where dust devils dance, whirling up into a wide, pale sky. Here you have no rain when all the earth cries for it, or quick downpours called cloud-bursts for violence. A land of lost rivers, with little in it to love; yet a land that once visited must be come back to inevitably. If it were not so there would be little told of it.

This is the country of three seasons. From June on to November it lies hot, still, and unbearable, sick with violent unrelieving storms; then on until April, chill, quiescent, drinking its scant rain and scanter snows; from April to the hot season again, blossoming, radiant, and seductive. These months are only approximate; later or earlier the rain-laden wind may drift up the water gate of the Colorado from the Gulf, and the land sets its seasons by the rain.

The desert floras shame us with their cheerful adaptations to the seasonal limitations. Their whole duty is to flower and fruit, and they do it hardly, or with tropical luxuriance, as the rain admits. It is recorded in the report of the Death Valley expedition that after a year of abundant rains, on the Colorado desert was found a specimen of Amaranthus ten feet high. A year later the same species in the same place matured in the drought at four inches. One hopes the land may breed like qualities in her human offspring, not tritely to "try," but to do. Seldom does the desert herb attain the full stature of the type. Extreme aridity and extreme altitude have the same dwarfing effect, so that we find in the high Sierras and in Death Valley related species in miniature that reach a comely growth in mean temperatures. Very fertile are the desert plants in expedients to prevent evaporation, turning their foliage edge-wise toward the sun, growing silky hairs, exuding viscid gum. The wind, which has a long sweep, harries and helps them. It rolls up dunes about the stocky stems, encompassing and protective, and above the dunes, which may be, as with the mesquite, three times as high as a man, the blossoming twigs flourish and bear fruit.

There are many areas in the desert where drinkable water lies within a few feet of the surface, indicated by the mesquite and the bunch grass [Sporobolus airoides]. It is this nearness of unimagined help that makes the tragedy of desert deaths. It is related that the final breakdown of that hapless party that gave Death Valley its forbidding name occurred in a locality where shallow wells would have saved them. But how were they to know that? Properly equipped it is possible to go safely across that ghastly sink, yet every year it takes its toll of death, and yet men find there sun-dried mummies, of whom no trace or recollection is preserved. To underestimate one's thirst, to pass a given landmark to the right or left, to find a dry spring where one looked for running water—there is no help for any of these things.

* * *

You should hear Salty Williams tell how he used to drive eighteen and twenty-mule teams from the borax marsh to Mojave, ninety miles, with the trail wagon full of water barrels. Hot days the mules would go so mad for drink that the clank of the water bucket set them into an uproar of hideous, maimed noises, and a tangle of harness chains, while Salty would sit on the high seat with the sun glare heavy in his eyes, dealing out curses of pacification in a level, uninterested voice until the clamor fell off from sheer exhaustion. There was a line of shallow graves along that road; they used to count on dropping a man or two of every new gang of coolies brought out in the hot season. But when he lost his swamper, smitten without warning at the noon halt, Salty quit his job; he said it was "too durn hot." The swamper he buried by the way with stones upon him to keep the coyotes from digging him up, and seven years later I read the penciled lines on the pine head-board, still bright and unweathered.

But before that, driving up on the Mojave stage, I met Salty again crossing Indian Wells, his face from the high seat, tanned and ruddy as a harvest moon, looming through the golden dust above his eighteen mules. The land had called him.

The palpable sense of mystery in the desert air breeds fables, chiefly of lost treasure. Somewhere within its stark borders, if one believes report, is a hill strewn with nuggets; one seamed with virgin silver; an old clayey water-bed where Indians scooped up earth to make cooking pots and shaped them reeking with grains of pure gold. Old miners drifting about the desert edges, weathered into the semblance of the tawny hills, will tell you tales like these convincingly. After a little sojourn in that land you will believe them on their own account. It is a question whether it is not better to be bitten by the little horned snake of the desert that goes sidewise and strikes without coiling, than by the tradition of a lost mine.

And yet—and yet—is it not perhaps to satisfy expectation that one falls into the tragic key in writing of desertness? The more you wish of it the more you get, and in the mean time lose much of pleasantness. In that country which begins at the foot of the east slope of the Sierras and spreads out by less and less lofty hill ranges toward the Great Basin, it is possible to live with great zest, to have red blood and delicate joys, to pass and repass about one's daily performance an area that would make an Atlantic seaboard State, and that with no peril, and, according to our way of thought, no particular difficulty. At any rate, it was not people who went into the desert merely to write it up who invented the fabled Hassaympa, of whose waters, if any drink, they can no more see fact as naked fact, but all radiant with the color of romance. I, who must have drunk of it in my twice seven years' wanderings, am assured that it is worth while.

For all the toll the desert takes of a man it gives compensations, deep breaths, deep sleep, and the communion of the stars. It comes upon one with new force in the pauses of the night that the Chaldeans were a desert-bred people. It is hard to escape the sense of mastery as the stars move in the wide clear heavens to risings and settings unobscured. They look large and near and palpitant; as if they moved on some stately service not needful to declare. Wheeling to their stations in the sky, they make the poor world-fret of no account. Of no account you who lie out there watching, nor the lean coyote that stands off in the scrub from you and howls and howls.

MARY HUNTER AUSTIN spent a dozen years exploring the California desert at the end of the 19th century and in 1903 published *The Land of Little Rain*, from which this essay is excerpted. She went on to write more than 30 books and became a prominent voice on water rights, Native American rights, women's suffrage and other issues. She died in 1934, and her home in Inyo County is a California Historical Landmark.

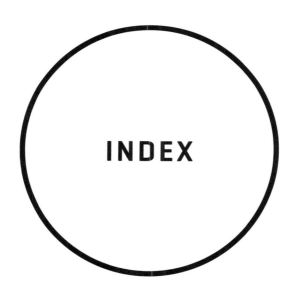

INDEX

INDEX

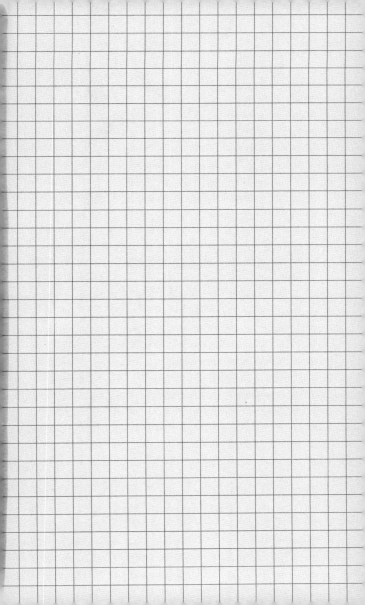